W9-CEI-195

FLANNERY O'CONNOR

FLANNERY O'CONNOR

LITERARY PROPHET OF THE SOUTH

Susan Balée

Chelsea House Publishers

New York • Philadelphia

CHELSEA HOUSE PUBLISHERS

EDITORIAL DIRECTOR   Richard Rennert
EXECUTIVE MANAGING EDITOR   Karyn Gullen Browne
COPY CHIEF   Robin James
PICTURE EDITOR   Adrian G. Allen
ART DIRECTOR   Robert Mitchell
MANUFACTURING DIRECTOR   Gerald Levine

GREAT ACHIEVERS: LIVES OF THE PHYSICALLY CHALLENGED

SENIOR EDITOR   Kathy Kuhtz Campbell
SERIES DESIGN   Basia Niemczyc

Staff for **FLANNERY O'CONNOR**
ASSOCIATE EDITOR   Martin Schwabacher
EDITORIAL ASSISTANT   Kelsey Goss
PICTURE RESEARCHER   Pat Burns
COVER ILLUSTRATION   Charles Lilly

First Printing

1 3 5 7 9 8 6 4 2

Library of Congress Cataloging-in-Publication Data

Balée, Susan.
Flannery O'Connor / Susan Balée.
p. cm.—(Great achievers: lives of the physically challenged)
Includes bibliographical references and index.
ISBN 0-7910-2418-0.
     0-7910-2419-9 (pbk.)   BT 18.95/15.16 - 4/95
1. O'Connor, Flannery—Biography—Juvenile literature. 2. Women authors, Ameri-
can—20th century—Biography—Juvenile literature. 3. Systemic lupus erythemato-
sus—Patients—United States—Biography—Juvenile literature. [1. O'Connor,
Flannery. 2. Authors, American. 3. Women—Biography. 4. Lupus—Patients.] I.
Title. II. Series: Great achievers (Chelsea House Publishers)
PS3565.C57Z582 1994   94-9377
813'.54—dc20   CIP
[B]   AC

CONTENTS

GREAT ACHIEVERS

LIVES OF THE PHYSICALLY CHALLENGED

A MESSAGE FOR EVERYONE

Jerry Lewis

Just 44 years ago—when I was the ripe old age of 23—an incredible stroke of fate rocketed me to overnight stardom as an entertainer. After the initial shock wore off, I began to have a very strong feeling that, in return for all life had given me, I must find a way of giving something back. At just that moment, a deeply moving experience in my personal life persuaded me to take up the leadership of a fledgling battle to defeat a then little-known group of diseases called muscular dystrophy, as well as other related neuromuscular diseases—all of which are disabling and, in the worst cases, cut life short.

In 1950, when the Muscular Dystrophy Association (MDA)—of which I am national chairman—was established, physical disability was looked on as a matter of shame. Franklin Roosevelt, who guided America through World War II from a wheelchair, and Harold Russell, the World War II hero who lost both hands in battle, then became an Academy Award–winning movie star and chairman of the President's Committee on Employment of the Handicapped, were the exceptions. One of the reasons that muscular dystrophy and related diseases were so little known was that people who had been disabled by them were hidden at home, away from the pity and discomfort with which they were generally regarded by society. As I got to know and began working with people who have disabilities, I quickly learned what a tragic mistake this perception was. And my determination to correct this terrible problem soon became as great as my commitment to see disabling neuromuscular diseases wiped from the face of the earth.

I have long wondered why it never occurs to us, as we experience the knee-jerk inclination to feel sorry for people who are physically disabled, that lives such as those led by President Roosevelt, Harold Russell, and all of the extraordinary people profiled in this Great Achievers series demonstrate unmistakably how wrong we are. Physical disability need not be something that blights life and destroys opportunity for personal fulfillment and accomplishment. On the contrary, as people such as Ray Charles, Stephen Hawking, and Ron Kovic prove, physical disability can be a spur to greatness rather than a condemnation of emptiness.

In fact, if my experience with physically disabled people can be taken as a guide, as far as accomplishment is concerned, they have a slight edge on the rest of us. The unusual challenges they face require finding greater-than-average sources of energy and determination to achieve much of what able-bodied people take for granted. Often, this ultimately translates into a lifetime of superior performance in whatever endeavor people with disabilities choose to pursue.

If you have watched my Labor Day Telethon over the years, you know exactly what I am talking about. Annually, we introduce to tens of millions of Americans people whose accomplishments would distinguish them regardless of their physical conditions—top-ranking executives, physicians, scientists, lawyers, musicians, and artists. The message I hope the audience receives is not that these extraordinary individuals have achieved what they have by overcoming a dreadful disadvantage that the rest of us are lucky not to have to endure. Rather, I hope our viewers reflect on the fact that these outstanding people have been ennobled and strengthened by the tremendous challenges they have faced.

In 1992, MDA, which has grown over the past four decades into one of the world's leading voluntary health agencies, established a personal achievement awards program to demonstrate to the nation that the distinctive qualities of people with disabilities are by no means confined to the famous. What could have been more appropriate or timely in that year of the implementation of the 1990 Americans with Disabilities Act than to take an action that could perhaps finally achieve the alteration of public perception of disability, which MDA had struggled over four decades to achieve?

On Labor Day, 1992, it was my privilege to introduce to America MDA's inaugural national personal achievement award winner, Steve Mikita, assistant attorney general of the state of Utah. Steve graduated magna cum laude from Duke University as its first wheelchair student in history and was subsequently named the outstanding young lawyer of the year by the Utah Bar Association. After he spoke on the Telethon with an eloquence that caused phones to light up from coast to coast, people asked me where he had been all this time and why they had not known of him before, so deeply impressed were they by him. I answered that he and thousands like him have been here all along. We just have not adequately *noticed* them.

It is my fervent hope that we can eliminate indifference once and for all and make it possible for all of our fellow citizens with disabilities to gain their rightfully high place in our society.

ON FACING CHALLENGES

John Callahan

I was paralyzed for life in 1972, at the age of 21. A friend and I were driving in a Volkswagen on a hot July night, when he smashed the car at full speed into a utility pole. He suffered only minor injuries. But my spinal cord was severed during the crash, leaving me without any feeling from my diaphragm downward. The only muscles I could move were some in my upper body and arms, and I could also extend my fingers. After spending a lot of time in physical therapy, it became possible for me to grasp a pen.

I've always loved to draw. When I was a kid, I made pictures of everything from Daffy Duck (one of my lifelong role models) to caricatures of my teachers and friends. I've always been a people watcher, it seems; and I've always looked at the world in a sort of skewed way. Everything I see just happens to translate immediately into humor. And so, humor has become my way of coping. As the years have gone by, I have developed a tremendous drive to express my humor by drawing cartoons.

The key to cartooning is to put a different spin on the expected, the normal. And that's one reason why many of my cartoons deal with the disabled: amputees, quadriplegics, paraplegics, the blind. The public is not used to seeing them in cartoons.

But there's another reason why my subjects are often disabled men and women. I'm sick and tired of people who presume to speak for the disabled. Call me a cripple, call me a gimp, call me paralyzed for life.

Just don't call me something I'm not. I'm not "differently abled," and my cartoons show that disabled people should not be treated any differently than anyone else.

All of the men, women, and children who are profiled in the Great Achievers series share this in common: their various handicaps have not prevented them from accomplishing great things. Their life stories are worth knowing about because they have found the strength and courage to develop their talents and to follow their dreams as fully as they can.

Whether able-bodied or disabled, a person must strive to overcome obstacles. There's nothing greater than to see a person who faces challenges and conquers them, regardless of his or her limitations.

Flannery O'Connor holds a copy of the newly published Wise Blood, *her first novel, in 1952. The novel caused a sensation in literary circles, but O'Connor felt that it was misunderstood by both supportive and critical reviewers.*

1

HOME TO ROOST

ON A MELLOW OCTOBER DAY in 1952, Flannery O'Connor stepped out onto the front porch of Andalusia, the farm where she lived with her mother on the outskirts of Milledgeville, Georgia. Looking down the hill from the wide, screened porch of the white farmhouse, the 26-year-old writer's bespectacled gaze took in the lawn that sloped down to the Eatonton-Atlanta highway and the small valley with a pond that lay beyond the road. The driveway to the O'Connor house cut through a bank of red clay and swerved around behind the farmhouse. The black farmhands lived back there, to the side a bit, in a darkly weathered farm building. The barn, with farm machinery sitting in its yard, sat beyond that.

As she waited for her mother to drive her to the train station in Milledgeville, Flannery listened happily to the bleat of 17 geese meandering by the porch in single file. In addition to the geese,

O'Connor had collected a flock of turkeys, another of mallard ducks, a pen of pheasants and quail, three Japanese silky bantams, two Polish Crested ones, and several chickens. Nevertheless, just that summer—when she learned that she had the fatal disease lupus and that she would spend the rest of her life on the farm—Flannery had felt something lacking in her aviary. What birds could she be missing? The answer: peacocks!

Against her mother's objections that they would eat all the flowers on the place, Flannery had ordered a pair of peafowl and four peabiddies from a breeder in Eustis, Florida. The birds had cost an expensive $65, but Flannery waited for them eagerly. At last they were scheduled to arrive at the Milledgeville train station, and she could bring them home to the dairy farm.

Regina O'Connor, Flannery's mother, joined her daughter on the porch. Regina, a formidable-looking woman who had managed the dairy farm herself since her husband's death, contrasted strongly in appearance with her frail daughter. Although both had a heart-shaped face and large eyes, their expressions were different. Mrs. O'Connor's set jaw bespoke determination, whereas Flannery's face tended to look glum and unhappy—unless, that is, something made her smile. Mrs. O'Connor still called her daughter Mary Flannery, though Flannery had dropped

Andalusia, the O'Connor family dairy farm, was successfully run by Flannery's mother, Regina, after Flannery's father's death. Flannery's peafowl destroyed the garden around the house, much to Regina's dismay.

the first name when she began to publish short stories. "Who was likely to buy the stories of an Irish washer-woman?" she once explained to a friend. As the pair drove the four miles into Milledgeville, the Georgia farmland gave way to white-columned mansions, large, well-tended green lawns, and gardens filled with azalea and dogwood. Milledgeville had been the capital of Georgia from 1807 to 1868, and its citizens still remembered the town's glory days during the "War Between the States" (the Civil War, 1861–65). The loss of that war continued to echo in the personality of the town and its people, and O'Connor wove it subtly into her stories and novels. When people asked her why there were so many good Southern writers, she would quote a line from the Alabama novelist Walker Percy: "Because we lost the War." Her fiction, about loss and redemption, embraced both the Southern loss of the Civil War and her central theme of the Christian Fall and Redemption.

When Flannery and her mother arrived at the train station, the crate rested on the platform. From one end of it, a peacock's royal-blue neck and crested head protruded. The bird glanced around attentively. Flannery jumped out of the car and ran forward; the peacock immediately tucked his head back in the crate. Flannery was delighted with this first glimpse of her new pet—more delighted, perhaps, than she had been with the recent publication of her first book.

Just a few months before, in May, Flannery O'Connor's first novel, *Wise Blood,* had been published to wide acclaim, although some reviewers had seemed puzzled about what she had been trying to do in the book. O'Connor was frustrated by many readers' apparent refusal to take the novel's preoccupation with religious matters seriously. She wrote in a preface to a later edition of the book, "That belief in Christ is to some a matter of life and death has been a stumbling block for readers who would prefer to think it a matter of no great consequence." Nevertheless, her book in no way resembled a conventional religious text. As she told her readers, "The book was written with zest and, if possible, it should be read that way. It is a comic novel about a Christian *malgré lui* [in spite of himself], and as such, very serious, for all comic novels that are any good must be about matters of life and death."

Wise Blood tells the story of Hazel Motes of Eastrod, Tennessee, who has recently completed his stint in the U.S. Army. Hazel returns to Eastrod only to discover all the Moteses gone and Eastrod a ghost town. Stunned, he travels to a strange new city, Taulkinham, where he meets a "blind" preacher, Asa Hawks, and his daughter, Sabbath Lily. Hazel tries to free himself from recollections of his Christian fundamentalist upbringing and from the sense that he is destined to become a preacher. To fight against this destiny, he founds "The Church Without Christ," and he soon has a disciple: a dim-witted youth named Enoch Emery.

Enoch steals a mummy from a museum and presents it to Hazel as a "new jesus." After delivering the new jesus, Enoch feels he deserves a reward and steals a gorilla costume, thinking that when he puts it on, everyone will want to shake his hand. There are other characters in the book, including many false preachers such as Asa, who serve as alter egos, or doubles, for Hazel. As Hazel's sense of unredeemed guilt deepens, he kills one of these characters, running over him with his car. Hazel then does penance by blinding himself with quicklime, wrapping barbed wire around his chest, and walking in shoes filled with rocks and broken glass. In the end, a policeman beats him to death with a billy club.

Not surprisingly, many reviewers were astonished by this strange novel. John W. Simons, writing in the June 27, 1952, issue of *Commonweal,* an eminent literary magazine, noted that *Wise Blood* was "a remarkably accomplished, remarkably precocious beginning" for a young writer. He called it "an important addition to the grotesque literature of Southern decadence." Sylvia Stallings, writing in the *New York Herald Tribune Book Review,* said that "the power of Miss O'Connor's writing comes from her understanding of the anguish of a mind tormented by God," but she wondered, "after an opening performance like this one, [where has she] left herself to go?" Some reviewers, however, were simply offended by the book. They could not understand the point of its violence, its weird and comic characters. Such critics tended to label her book with what had become, for Southern writers, derogatory terms: They called *Wise Blood* a "Southern gothic" novel, or, simply, "grotesque."

Flannery O'Connor found herself trying to explain and defend her fiction. The Northern critics who insulted her work particularly offended her, and she observed, "If you are a Southern writer, that label, and all the misconceptions that go with it, is pasted on you at once, and you are left to get it off as best you can." Nevertheless, she agreed that Southern fiction often had a peculiar quality about it—the combination of horror and humor, of characters both violent and comic—that could be described as "grotesque." She also noted, though, that a great deal of Southern fiction simply got lumped into the category: "Of course, I have found that anything that comes out of the South is going to be called grotesque by the Northern reader, unless it is grotesque, in which case it's going to be called realistic."

In her own work, however, Flannery purposely drew grotesque characters to show humankind's moral deformity in the modern world. She observed, "Whenever I'm asked why Southern writers particularly have a penchant for writing about freaks, I say it is because we are still able to recognize one." She explained that Southerners, because they lived in the Bible Belt—a region steeped in religious belief—could recognize the fallen state of human nature and describe sinners as they really appeared. "I hate to think," she said, "that in twenty years Southern writers too may be writing about men in gray-flannel suits and may have lost their ability to see that these gentlemen are even greater freaks than what we are writing about now."

In Milledgeville, though people may not have understood her book, they were proud of their young novelist. Flannery became the toast of the town—the city's new "literary lion." The young writer felt obliged to order many extra copies of her novel because "my nine copies have to go to a set of relatives who are waiting anxiously to condemn the book until they get a free copy." Relatives, friends, and well-wishers insisted on giving her parties, to which she felt compelled to go. She wrote to a fellow novelist with a book about to be released, "I hope you won't have as much trouble about keeping people from having parties for you as I am having. Around here if you publish the number of whiskers on the local pigs, everybody has to give you a tea."

For the most part, though, Flannery stuck close to the family farm and to her solitary pursuits of writing, painting, and watching her birds. During the summer and fall of 1952, she was adapting to the fact that she would spend the rest of her life in Milledgeville. Before this she had ventured away from home to earn a master of fine arts degree at the Iowa Writers' Workshop, and then she had lived in New York and Connecticut. She had been happiest living in Connecticut with her friends, the family of poet and translator Robert Fitzgerald, but pain in the joints in late December 1950 sent her home to Milledgeville to see her doctor. When she arrived, feverish and in great pain, her mother immediately took her to the local hospital. The doctor soon confirmed—but only to Regina O'Connor— that Flannery was dying of lupus erythematosus, an incurable disease in which the body's immune system attacks its own vital tissues. Flannery had inherited lupus erythematosus from her father, who died of the disease in 1941. Mrs. O'Connor, however, feared to tell her daughter the nature of her illness. Instead, she told Flannery that she was suffering from rheumatoid arthritis.

Flannery remained many weeks in the hospital, finishing *Wise Blood* and writing letters to friends, including the one to Betty Boyd Love excerpted below:

> I am languishing on my bed of semi affliction, this time with AWTHRITUS or, to give it all it has, *the* acute rheumatoid arthritis, what leaves you always willing to sit down, lie down, lie flatter, etc. But I am taking cortisone so I will have to get up again. These days you caint even have you a good psychosomatic ailment to get yourself a rest. I will be in Milledgeville Ga. a bird sanctuary for a few months, waiting to see how much of an invalid I am going to get to be. At Christmas the horsepital is full of old rain crows & tree frogs only— & accident victims— & me, but I don't believe in time no more much so it's all one to me.

Flannery's humorous tone here belies her very real suffering. Fevers caused her hair to fall out, and the cortisone made her face swell. Her doctor, Arthur Merrill,

O'Connor wrote that when a peacock shows his tail "you will see in a green-bronze arch around him a galaxy of gazing, haloed suns," adding, "this is the moment when most people are silent." At one time she had more than 40 peafowl.

O'Connor (seated) attends an autograph party in May 1952 celebrating the publication of Wise Blood *shortly before she became ill with what was later diagnosed as lupus.*

warned Mrs. O'Connor that her daughter might die. Despite this grim prognosis, Flannery finally left the hospital in March 1951, moving with her mother from their house in town to Andalusia, where she took a bedroom on the ground floor because she did not have the strength to climb the stairs. In addition to her regime of writing three hours every morning, Flannery now had to learn to give herself daily shots of cortisone and maintain a rigorously salt-free diet.

In 1951, however, the young writer still had hopes of returning to live with the Fitzgeralds in Connecticut. In June 1952, she finally realized that this would be impossible. During a five-week visit to her friends, a viral infection reactivated her lupus, and Flannery was forced to return to Georgia. At this time she finally learned that she was not suffering from rheumatoid arthritis but had inherited her father's lupus. This bout with the disease required another hospital visit, two blood transfusions, and a six-week stay in bed. It was at this point that Flannery wrote the Fitzgeralds, asking them to send the books and clothing she had left there in December 1950. It was also the month she ordered her first pair of peafowl from the breeder in Florida. These were the birds that finally arrived in October, that Flannery and her mother had driven to the Milledgeville train station to retrieve.

The O'Connors, mother and daughter, brought the birds back to the farm late in the afternoon. They uncrated the peacocks in a pen because the breeder had written Flannery that she should keep them penned up for a week or so, only letting them out at dusk in the place where she wanted them to roost. Flannery sat down in awe on the now-empty crate and studied her regal birds. Even without a tail (the peacock sheds his tail in late summer and does not regain it completely until the new year), the cock strutted as if he had a full train behind him. These birds, like Flannery, had come home to roost permanently in Milledgeville.

Flannery had accepted the fact that she would live the rest of her life in the small Southern town, studying the habits of its people and its peafowl, and writing fiction. "I intend to stand firm and let the peacocks multiply," she wrote, "for I am sure that, in the end, the last word will be theirs." In the end, however, the last word was Flannery O'Connor's. She found at home rich material for her stories and novels—her fiction portrayed the lives of the religious and the antireligious Southerners, the clashes of the classes in Southern society, and the physical features of her native Georgia—and composed what became some of America's most meaningful and compelling literature of the 20th century.

Mary Flannery O'Connor, age seven, is seen here in a photograph commemorating her First Communion. Although the Roman Catholic community in Georgia was small, she never felt ostracized because of her religion, which was a source of comfort to her and provided rich material for her stories.

2

A CATHOLIC
IN THE SOUTH

MARY FLANNERY O'CONNOR was born in Savannah, Georgia, on March 25, 1925. The only child of Regina Cline O'Connor and Edward Francis O'Connor, Jr., Flannery entered at birth into Savannah's minority Roman Catholic community. The history of the Catholics in Savannah is entwined in the history of the city itself—the oldest and once the most sophisticated city in Georgia.

Savannah was founded by James Oglethorpe in 1733 and later figured prominently in both the Revolutionary War and the Civil War, falling to enemy forces in both. However, for much of the 18th and 19th centuries Savannah rivaled Charleston, South Carolina, as the most prosperous of the Southern ports. Like other southern colonies, Georgia reaped the economic benefits of slave labor. In Savannah, a small but powerful ruling class—the white plantation owners—built themselves opulent houses in both the country and the city. They earned vast sums of money harvesting crops such as rice, indigo, and, farther inland, cotton, which they traded for huge profits in the West Indies and England.

Despite Georgia's hot and muggy climate, these plantation owners often lived like European aristocracy, purchasing their clothes and the furnishings of their houses from England and France. In the years before the Revolutionary War, a typical Savannah aristocrat would dress himself, his wife, and his children in ornate silks and satins; carry his toothpicks in a silver case; drink fine Madeira wine from a crystal decanter; keep time with an exquisitely designed hourglass; and while away his hours dancing, playing cards, or listening to his lady playing sonatas on a spinet. He would probably collect European paintings for his home and fill its rooms with expensive mahogany and walnut furniture—imported from England. Very often a well-educated man, he would read books borrowed from the Library Society of Savannah and philosophize with his friends about the latest advances in science and the arts.

Meanwhile, the slaves who worked his fields and earned him his fortune had none of his possessions and would not have even their freedom for nearly another century. In the Civil War, fought to unite the nation and free the slaves, Savannah fell to the Northern general, William Tecumseh Sherman. After setting fire to Atlanta on November 14, 1864, Sherman marched across the state to Savannah. He burned millions of dollars worth of property during his campaign across Georgia, destroying whatever his soldiers could not eat or carry off. He reached Savannah in December, and the city surrendered to him without a struggle. On December 22, Sherman sent a message to President Lincoln: "I beg to present you as a Christmas Gift the City of Savannah, with 150 heavy guns and plenty of ammunition, also about 25,000 bales of cotton."

At the time of Flannery O'Connor's birth in 1925, the War Between the States was long over, but its legacy lived on in the memories of the citizens of Savannah. For instance, her cousin Katie, who lived next door and strongly influenced Flannery all of her life, was the daughter of Captain John Flannery, who had fought for the Confederacy. Katie's husband, Raphael Semmes, was the nephew of a well-known Confederate naval commander. These people remembered the prosperity of the antebellum (before the war) South, but had lived into the hard times of the 20th century.

Savannah in the 1920s had decidedly lost its former prosperity. The port that had once been filled with bales of cotton was empty of goods now—boll weevils in the cotton crop had been ruining Georgia farmers since 1915. The once-shouted slogan "Cotton Is King" had lost its ring by the mid-1920s. But Savannah at that time had no other industries to compensate for the loss of the cotton trade.

The city still had its distinguished history, its aristocratic houses, and its famous design—the entire city is laid out in squares, the original idea of James Oglethorpe when he first founded the city—but it also had racial and economic divisions. Blacks and whites were segregated socially, residentially, and educationally. Flannery O'Connor would have seen few blacks in her childhood other than those who worked as servants in the households of her white neighbors. Blacks continued to languish on the lowest level of Georgia's society and economy, even though the Emancipation Proclamation had freed them more than six decades earlier.

Flannery's family, though white and prosperous enough, had also experienced discrimination. They were Catholic, and Catholics had suffered in Georgia. Indeed, although Savannah supported a large Catholic population in the 1920s, the city and the state had been founded with a charter that banned Catholicism. Nevertheless, Catholicism came to Georgia when the first Irish immigrants arrived. Far down the social scale from the aristocratic plantation owners, the first Irish who came to the city arrived as indentured servants, and their status was not much higher than that of the enslaved blacks when they stepped off the boat. After working off their debts, however, these Irish Catholic indentured servants could buy their freedom in Georgia, and a large population of them stayed right in Savannah.

After the Revolutionary War, Catholics in Savannah had more rights, but they continued to be harassed long into the 20th century. Just a few years before Flannery was born, the Convent Inspection Bill became law in Georgia. This bill permitted Georgia authorities to search the living quarters of nuns, looking for evidence of "immorality"— something that many Protestant Georgians believed they would find there. The 1920s saw a resurgence of the Ku Klux Klan, the white supremacists who, disguised in their white robes and pointed caps, persecuted blacks in the South. During this same era—and undoubtedly by some of these same people—Roman Catholics also endured harassment.

For this reason, Catholics in Savannah had segregated themselves from Protestants. They lived in their own parts of town, and Flannery's house stood in the center of Savannah's most Catholic quarter, Lafayette Square. On the other side of the square from the O'Connor townhouse, the Gothic spires of the Cathedral of St. John the Baptist still rise high into the air. Every Sunday the O'Connors attended mass at St. John's. When she turned six, Flannery started school at St. Vincent's Grammar School, a Catholic girls' school located between the cathedral and her house. She spent 5 years at St. Vincent's, and 12 in the deeply Catholic atmosphere of her neighborhood and family.

One can imagine the effect this childhood had on Flannery as a writer, because she spoke of it later in an essay, "The Catholic Novelist in the Protestant South":

> The things we see, hear, smell, and touch affect us long before we believe anything at all, and the South impresses its image on us from the moment we are able to distinguish

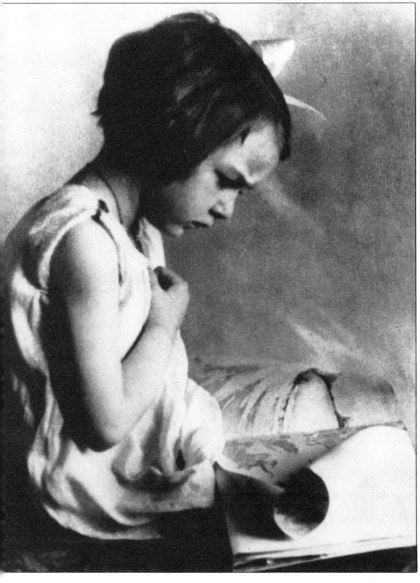

Mary Flannery concentrates on a book. Even as a child her writing had acerbic flair; a journal kept when she was 12 warns away snoopers with "I know some folks that don't mind their own business."

one sound from another. By the time we are able to use our imaginations for fiction, we find that our senses have responded irrevocably to a certain reality.

Flannery's childhood reality in Savannah included daily prayers and hymns, church bells and incense, and later, Communion and confession. At St. Vincent's, Flannery learned her catechism—a formal set of questions and answers about the Catholic church and its doctrines. Here is one of the most basic question-and-answer exchanges from the catechism:

Q: "Who made you?"
A: "God made me."
Q: "Why did God make you?"
A: "To know Him, to love Him, and to serve Him in this world and the next."

Flannery and her classmates did more than memorize correct answers to set questions, however. They were also taught secular subjects—reading, writing, and math.

This aerial view shows the Cathedral of St. John the Baptist on Lafayette Square, Savannah's most Catholic quarter. The Gothic spires of the church, where the O'Connors attended mass every Sunday, can be seen from the porch of Flannery's childhood home.

(Though she was destined to grow up to be a renowned writer, Flannery's lowest grades were always in spelling.) Some of her former classmates at St. Vincent's, interviewed in February 1990 by Hugh R. Brown of Armstrong State College, recalled that Flannery sometimes irritated the nuns who taught her. They remember Flannery as being "a little forward with adults," speaking to them as if she were on their level. She also annoyed her writing instructor, Sister Mary Consolata, with her many compositions about chickens and ducks. The sister finally banned essays on this theme, although Flannery had achieved national fame as a five-year-old when her chicken appeared on Pathé News, the New York newsreel company whose short news features often preceded movies in theaters.

Flannery had trained one of her chickens, a Cochin Bantam, to walk backward, and its fame spread in the press until finally the newsreel photographer arrived in Savannah to record this feat. Many years later Flannery noted, "by the time she reached the attention of Pathé News, I suppose there was nowhere left for [the chicken] to go—forward or backward. Shortly after that she died, as now seems fitting."

Despite the sister's ban on "fowl" compositions, young Flannery continued to write often and to read extensively. Already a literary critic as a small child, she wrote her responses to books on their inside covers. She thought Louisa May Alcott's *Little Men* "first rate. Splendid," but scribbled in Lewis Carroll's *Alice in Wonderland*, "Awful. I wouldn't read this book." In the flyleaf of a popular children's book of the period, Shirley Watkin's *Georgia Finds Herself*, Flannery wrote, "This is the worst book I ever read next to 'Pinnochio.'"

Flannery's mother, Regina O'Connor, kept a close eye on her daughter's upbringing. Mrs. O'Connor walked her daughter to and from school at St. Vincent's, though it was 30 yards from the house, and she kept a list of approved playmates for her child. One childhood friend remembers an afternoon when an approved playmate arrived at the O'Connor house with an unapproved playmate in tow. The unapproved child was promptly sent home.

When Flannery was 11, Mrs. O'Connor enrolled her in Sacred Heart, a parochial school two miles away from St. Vincent's. Many people remember Flannery's days at that school, for she arrived in a conspicuous fashion: Mrs. O'Connor drove her over in an electric car owned by Cousin Katie. The car was a large convertible and Mrs. O'Connor drove it wearing a veil, duster, and long gloves. A vase of flowers graced the dashboard, and Mary Flannery rode in the passenger seat. Sister M. Jude Walsh of Savannah, a third-grader at the time, remembers that the car "was kind of like the Toonerville trolley. A group of us would stand on the corner every day to see Mary Flannery arrive, and we'd be there at 2:15 to see her leave."

When not at school, Flannery O'Connor played mainly at her own house rather than at the playground two blocks away. She did not visit other children, either, though she occasionally ventured downtown to see a movie with a friend. Usually, however, Flannery invited friends to her house, and they played in the backyard with the chickens and ducks, as well as in a large playhouse that Katie Semmes had built for her favorite little cousin. On Saturday mornings Flannery would listen with relatives to a popular radio show, "Let's Pretend," followed by ginger-bread cookies for all.

Although very little is known about Flannery O'Connor's relationship with her father, it is clear that he was proud of his precocious daughter. Later in her life Flannery recollected to a friend that her father carried around her "early productions" in the pocket of his coat, showing these drawings and scraps of verse to his friends. When she was two years old, Mr. O'Connor paid for her to have a separate telephone listing in the city directory—a distinction that lasted until 1931. In 1936, when she was 11, Flannery was also listed as a contributor to the Female

Regina Cline O'Connor poses with Mary Flannery, age two. Regina was an extremely protective mother who kept close tabs on her rambunctious child.

Orphanage Society in the Catholic paper, though her parents' names do not appear.

From these small facts it seems evident that Mr. O'Connor had both a whimsical sense of humor and a great fondness for his only child. But what is actually known

Flannery attended St. Vincent's Grammar School for five years. It is seen here in the 1940s after it became a community service center.

about Flannery's father consists mainly of an outline of events. He was the great-grandson of one of Savannah's many Irish immigrants, a wheelwright named Patrick O'Connor who founded a stable and wagon-making business in the city. Edward O'Connor was born in 1896 and served as an infantry lieutenant in France during World War I. In 1922, he married Flannery's mother, Regina Cline.

After his discharge from the army Edward worked for his father, a wholesale distributor of tobacco and candy. But before Flannery was born, he went into the real estate business—unsuccessfully. He bought the townhouse on Lafayette Square in 1923, but conveyed it to Cousin Katie for a debt deed of $4,500 soon after. When the family moved to Atlanta in 1938, he had not yet paid the debt. In fact, Cousin Katie owned the house until her death, when she left it to Flannery.

In the 1930s, Edward O'Connor gave up on self-employment after a series of his companies failed in Savannah. In 1938, plagued by debt, he accepted a post with the Federal Housing Administration (FHA) in Atlanta, and the family moved away from the city of Flannery's birth.

Leaving Savannah was difficult for the 12-year-old Flannery. After spending the spring of 1938 in Atlanta, she moved with her mother to the Cline family home in Milledgeville. The Clines, Flannery's mother's family, had a long and distinguished history in Milledgeville.

The Cline House, built in 1820, with its grand portico, exhibits the traditional style of the antebellum South.

Regina's great-grandfather, Peter Cline, came from Ireland in 1845. An educated man, when he first arrived in the United States he taught Latin at a school in Augusta, Georgia. His son, Peter James Cline, became a prosperous merchant and acquired a great deal of property in and around Milledgeville. In 1888, he was elected the city's first Catholic mayor. Cline married first Kate L. Treanor, and then Margaret Ida, her sister, after Kate died. His first wife gave him seven children, and his second wife gave him nine—Regina was the seventh child by his second wife. The house to which Flannery and her mother moved in 1938 had first been purchased by Regina's remarkable father in 1886, but it had been originally built in 1820.

The house is a good example of Southern antebellum architecture, with its four white, fluted columns rising above the entryway to the second story and its many porticos, gables, and windows. Slaves originally built a brick wall around this house, marking off the garden. Dogwood and lavender filled the lush garden when Flannery moved there with her mother. Across the garden from the Cline House, the nearest neighboring structure was the Governor's Mansion, a historic building that had been Governor Joseph Brown's house during the days when Milledgeville was the capital of Georgia. General Sherman, on his march to the coast, stopped briefly in this mansion, but Brown and his confederate legislature had already fled to Macon. For some reason Sherman spared the mansion, but he is reported to have poured molasses into the organ of the nearby Presbyterian church.

During Flannery's first year in Milledgeville her father continued to live in Atlanta, where he worked. His health was growing worse, however. Two years before, in 1936, he was told he had arthritis. But doctors had recently revised Edward O'Connor's diagnosis, and he was told that he suffered from the deadly disease lupus erythematosus. In 1939, the film version of *Gone with the Wind* premiered in Atlanta and became one of the all-time great

When Flannery's father, Edward Francis O'Connor, pictured here, died of lupus in 1941, the O'Connors were told the disease was not passed on from parent to child, but Flannery's subsequent illness proved that assumption wrong.

social events in Georgia history (an event Flannery would later refer to in her short story, "A Late Encounter with the Enemy"). But Flannery's father's deteriorating health was the main concern of the O'Connor household. In 1939, his condition became so serious that he resigned from his job with the FHA and retired to Milledgeville to live with his wife and daughter.

On February 1, 1941, Edward Francis O'Connor died of lupus and was buried in the family plot in Milledgeville. The death of her father so deeply shocked the 15-year-old Flannery that afterward she could rarely bring herself to speak of him. Yet it would be only 10 years before she discovered that she had inherited her father's fatal disease.

O'Connor (right) works on the Corinthian, *the quarterly literary magazine of Georgia State College for Women. O'Connor edited the magazine during her senior year.*

3

THE PRECOCIOUS
STUDENT

FLANNERY O'CONNOR GRADUATED from Milledgeville's Peabody High School in 1942, during the first year of America's involvement in World War II. (America had entered the war on December 8, 1941, the day after Japanese airplanes bombed Pearl Harbor.) Throughout 1942 war raged in Europe, Africa, and the South Pacific. Americans defeated the Japanese at Midway in the Pacific and drove the German general Rommel from North Africa. During this year in Europe the Nazis began the systematic murder of millions of Jews in concentration-camp gas chambers. In America, the government began rationing staples, such as sugar, gasoline, and coffee.

In Flannery's home state of Georgia, thousands of men volunteered for the navy, the marines, the army, and the Army Air Corps (now the U.S. Air Force). All told, more than 320,000 Georgians served, and 6,754 were killed or listed as missing in action by the end of the war.

The governor of Georgia, Ellis Arnall, updated the 1877 constitution in 1942 to benefit the youngest soldiers, changing the legal voting age from 21 to 18. The new constitution also carefully avoided all references to the "white primary"—a voting system that permitted only the votes of whites to count toward elections and effectively disenfranchised black Georgians from having a voice in politics. The U.S. Supreme Court had already begun its attack on the white primary, and as Flannery O'Connor's first published stories would emphasize, the position of black Southerners had begun its slow shift upward during the 1940s.

As Flannery began her freshman year at Georgia State College for Women (today Georgia College)—a block from her house in Milledgeville—other Southern writers were achieving national fame. In 1942, Ellen Glasgow, a novelist from Richmond, Virginia, received the Pulitzer Prize for *In This Our Life.* In the same year, Mississippi's William Faulkner published *Go Down, Moses,* his acclaimed collection of short stories. Flannery contributed stories and poems to her college literary magazine, the *Corinthian,* and cartoons to the college paper, *Colonnade.*

O'Connor's personality in college was marked by the same offbeat wit that had distinguished her in Peabody High School. One of her teachers remembered the highly original manner in which she fulfilled the final requirement of a high school home-economics course. The assignment had been "to make an original article of clothing for herself or a child relative." While the other students sewed in class, Flannery appeared to dawdle, doing nothing. On the day the final outfits were due,

> the other projects were laid out on tables ready for the teacher's examination. But no Flannery. The instructor, gradebook in hand, started her inspection of the dainty lace offerings when the door opened and in came the missing student, calm and unhurried, followed by a bantam hen, who frisked along attired in a handmade white

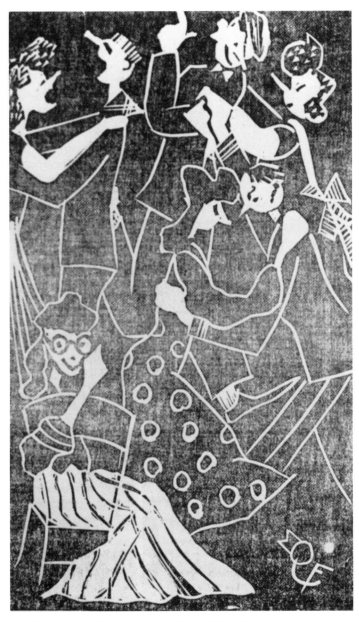

One of O'Connor's cartoons, captioned "Oh well. I can always be a Ph.D.," appeared in the 1943 issue of the Colonnade, *a college newspaper. O'Connor always disliked formal social events, which she found boring and forced.*

piqué coat with a belt at the back. (That hen, it turned out, also had an elegant pair of striped trousers.)

Despite her reputation as a wit, however, O'Connor took no part in social mixers or dances in high school, or later at college. One of her undergraduate cartoons seems to comment on her sense of herself as a wallflower. The cartoon depicts a girl who looks like O'Connor wearing big eyeglasses and sitting by herself at a dance while couples spin all around her. The girl's smile looks rather forced and the caption reads: "Oh well, I can always be a Ph.D."

Although O'Connor did go on to graduate school, it was to receive a master of fine arts in creative writing rather than a Ph.D. (doctor of philosophy). As for her love life, very little is known about it. In 1943, she met a marine sergeant named John Sullivan who was stationed at the college naval base. He became a dear friend and frequent

These endpapers, drawn in 1945 by O'Connor for the college newspaper the Spectrum, *show students trying to cope with mud, construction, and congestion on campus. O'Connor enjoyed cartooning and even sent some of her drawings to the* New Yorker, *which turned them down.*

visitor to the Milledgeville house; in 1944, when he was transferred to the Pacific, she wrote him regularly. None of these letters, however, has yet been published, so it is hard to estimate the nature of their relationship. In 1946, when the war ended and Sullivan received his discharge from the navy, he entered a seminary to become a priest. After that event O'Connor's correspondence with him gradually ended.

During her time at Georgia State College for Women, however, Flannery made many enduring female friends, most notably Betty Boyd Love, with whom she corresponded for the rest of her life. In the years that followed, as a local celebrity and alumna, she regularly accepted invitations to lecture at the college, though she hated the pretentiousness of these occasions and the inevitable tea parties and receptions that preceded and followed them. In 1956, she became friends with the playwright Maryat Lee, whose brother had recently become president of the college. In a 1957 letter to Lee, Flannery describes the aftermath of one of her college lectures as a "famous alumna":

> Last Friday week I stood in a receiving line with your brother and sister-in-law for a good hour, pressing the soggy paws of citizens from all over the state who have daughters in college. Your sister-in-law is a whiz bang at it. The guests had their names pinned on them and she never failed to see the name and say it. As for me, my eye was as glazed as the one on the fish served . . .

Flannery impressed her teachers and fellow students during her undergraduate years at Georgia State College for Women. She excelled in her English courses and had already begun to write promising short stories, which she published in the *Corinthian*. By her senior year she had become the editor of that magazine and set forth the new staff policy in an editorial entitled "Excuse Us While We Don't Apologize." In her editorial she noted that a student

Betty Boyd Love became a lifelong friend of O'Connor's after the two met at Georgia State College for Women. O'Connor and Love exchanged letters monthly after they graduated, Flannery setting out for Iowa to study writing and Betty leaving for North Carolina to study mathematics.

writer usually tries to please three audiences: students, faculty, and herself. But, the new editor observed:

> We on the *Corinthian* staff this year think we will be different. We are agreed that we will be just as bad as all previous staff members—but we will be different. Although the majority of you like the "my love has gone now I shall moan" type of work, we will give you none of it. Although the minority of you prefer consistent punctuation and a smack of literary pretension, we aren't going to worry about giving it to you.

> In short, we will write as we feel, preserving a modicum of orthodox English and making a small effort at keeping our originality out of our spelling. Some of us will strive for Art, some of us for free publicity, and some, the wiser of us by far, will not strive.

> If you like what we do, that's very nice.

If you don't, please remember the paper drive when you dispose of your copy.

—The Editor

Whenever she discussed her work in the years that followed, O'Connor continued to be as honest as she had been in this early statement. Neither her honesty nor her sense of humor ever failed her, and both of them distinguish her art.

As her college career closed, George Beiswanger, one of the professors she had impressed, seriously encouraged her to apply to the University of Iowa's graduate writing program—considered then, as now, the best creative writing program in America. Flannery applied for and won a scholarship in journalism that paid both her tuition and a stipend of $65 per term. Paul Engle, director of the Iowa Writers' Workshop, accepted her on the basis of her submitted short stories. He described them as "imaginative, tough, alive," as well as "filled with insight about human weakness, hard and compassionate." When he first met her, however, Engle could not understand her thick Southern accent, and part of their initial conversation was conducted on a notepad. Engle maintained that the other students would share his difficulty, and throughout her tenure in the writing program he read her stories aloud to the class for her.

In addition to writing classes Flannery studied literature, advanced drawing, American political cartooning, magazine writing, and advertising. She enjoyed her fellow students, with whom she shared meals and conversations and more interests than she had with most of the Southern belles who were her classmates at Georgia State College for Women. Flannery wrote to her mother every day, and her mother sent her daily copies of the Milledgeville newspaper. In 1946, at 21, she sold her first short story, "The Geranium," to *Accent* magazine. The story treats themes that Flannery would return to throughout her career—themes of displacement and homesickness, particularly of the Southerner displaced to another region of America, and of country people displaced in cityscapes.

"The Geranium" is the story of Old Dudley, a Georgian from a county outside of Atlanta, who has moved to New York City to live with his daughter and son-in-law. Old Dudley has come to the city on a whim—because he was getting old, because his daughter wanted him to be near "family," but mainly because he had seen a romanticized version of New York City in a movie, *Big Town Rhythm*. Once he arrives, however, he finds he hates the city. He is totally dependent on his daughter and feels trapped in her small apartment. Back in his boardinghouse in Coa County, he had been "the man of the house." He had also been the "master" of his black friend, Rabie, with whom he had fished and hunted. He had brought the fish home to the boardinghouse, where they provided meals for the

This part of the campus of the University of Iowa in Iowa City during the 1950s looks as it did when O'Connor attended the college 10 years earlier. Although O'Connor's accent gave her trouble at the Iowa Writers' Workshop, she enjoyed the opportunity to meet other writers and to polish her own work.

elderly female tenants who looked up to him as both provider and protector. Rabie looked up to him, too; Old Dudley could explain things to him, like the mechanical operation of guns.

In New York City, however, his daughter does not look up to him; she is exasperated by him. He feels claustrophobic in their high-rise apartment—the halls remind him of "dog runs," the people are unfriendly. The women do not talk to him, and the men leaning out their windows snarl at him if he stares. And he does stare, particularly at the window across the alley in which a geranium pot is set every morning. It is a displaced plant; barely tended, in a city window when it should be in a yard, like Old Dudley it subsists but cannot thrive.

The climactic scene in the story occurs when Old Dudley, on an errand for his daughter, begins to reminisce in the stairwell about hunting with Rabie. As he mimics the gestures of firing a rifle, a black neighbor—a Yankee—comes up the stairs. "What are you hunting, old timer?" the black man calls out, and Old Dudley is stunned; blacks in the South would never address a white man in such a familiar tone. He sinks to his knees in humiliation, and the black neighbor amiably helps him up the steps. Mortified and enraged, Old Dudley permits the man to lead him back to his daughter's door. Once inside, he goes immediately to the window and discovers that the geranium has fallen over the sill—it lies broken in the alley, six floors below. Old Dudley begins to cry and the geranium's owner laughs at him. One of the story's final images is of the dying geranium lying on the pavement with its roots in the air.

The most compelling aspect of this story is Old Dudley's reaction to the friendly black neighbor who he feels has insulted him. Old Dudley is a sympathetic character, but his attitude to the Northern black man is that of a white supremacist—he feels humiliated when the man speaks to him as an equal. Ironically, the person with whom he feels the most kinship in the South—more than he feels for his own daughter—is also a black man, Rabie. But this man plays a subordinate role to Old Dudley; he listens to what Dudley tells him and is politely subservient.

Flannery O'Connor was attempting in "The Geranium" to examine fairly the racial issues that had plagued Georgia since the days of slavery. Recent legislation in Georgia had exacerbated the conflicts between blacks and whites. In March 1946, when Flannery sold the story to *Accent,* a federal court in New Orleans declared the Georgia white primary illegal. Although this offered some hope of positive political change to black Georgians, it also intensified the white Georgians' fear and dislike of blacks. White racist politicians played on this fear, and Eugene Talmadge, who had consistently opposed opportunities for blacks in either the workplace or the classroom, won the governorship for a fourth time in 1946. He died before he could be inaugurated, but his son, Herman Talmadge, won the office in 1948 by using the same white supremacy scare tactics.

The Talmadges, unfortunately, were not radically different in their opinions on race from most white Georgians; this was why their antiblack rallying cry could elect them to the state's highest office. Southern blacks had suffered in America since the days of their enslavement. Even after the Thirteenth Amendment to the U.S. Constitution prohibited slavery, most blacks were still treated as second-class citizens in America. Degraded by the long denial of decent living conditions and access to education as well as by the deepest discrimination on the part of white Southerners, free blacks were not much better off after the Civil War than they had been as slaves before it. The notion of white supremacy and black inferiority continued to hold them down, and laws enforcing segregation of the races distanced them still further from true equality. Trains, steamboats, and public vehicles all had separate compartments for whites and blacks. On railway coaches blacks would often be forced to sit in second-class accommodations even if they held first-class tickets.

These laws that segregated blacks from whites were known as Jim Crow laws, and they intensified Southern racism. At the turn of the century, a series of ultraracist books appeared with titles such as *The Negro, a Beast* (1900) and *The Negro: A Menace to Civilization* (1907). The era of segregation and racism continued unabated until World War II, at which point the first feeble moves in the direction of equality began. It was hard to resurrect the fiction of white supremacy after large numbers of black and white men had fought together side by side.

Prior to the war, Southern blacks had most often responded to Jim Crow laws and customs by simply trying to endure them. In the face of overwhelming discrimination from a hostile white majority, they had little choice. Southern blacks earned wages one-fourth that of white workers and were barred from most labor unions; when black men could not find employment, their wives became maids and nannies to white families, often almost recreating the roles they had held as slaves in the antebellum South.

Many black Southerners responded to this dismal situation by leaving their homes and traveling North, where they hoped to encounter less racism. The black flight out of the South between the world wars is known as "the Great Migration." For blacks who remained in the South, however, subservience was the oil that lubricated all of their relations with whites. As Monroe Billington, a historian of the South, has observed, "Social contact, except when the Negro was clearly recognized to be in an inferior position, did not exist." This situation explains Old Dudley's difficulty in dealing with the Northern black man who assumes a familiarity with him that would be almost unthinkable in mid-1940s Georgia.

Flannery O'Connor, who recognized and wrote about the prejudice against blacks in the South, nevertheless

In the 1940s, black field-workers pick cotton missed by the mechanical pickers in the 1940s. Like many Southerners, O'Connor realized that race relations in the South, although still disadvantageous to blacks, were changing, and she explored the ramifications of those shifts in several of her stories.

understood the intricacies of the race problem. In this first published short story, "The Geranium," she tried to sketch the dilemma of the Old South confronted with the new, but in a later interview, she put it more explicitly:

[The Southerner's] social situation demands more of him than that elsewhere in the country. It requires considerable grace for two races to live together, particularly when the population is divided fifty-fifty between them and when they have a particular history. It can't be done without a code of manners based on mutual charity. . . . [The] old manners are obsolete, but the new manners will have to be based on what was best in the old ones—in this real basis of charity and necessity. . . . For the rest of the country, the race problem is solved when the Negro has his rights, but for the Southerner, whether he's white or colored, that's only the beginning. The South has to evolve a way of life in which the two races can live together with mutual forbearance. You don't form a committee to do this or pass a resolution; both races have to work it out the hard way.

Flannery O'Connor rewrote "The Geranium" in the 1960s and entitled it "Judgement Day." That story, which will be discussed later in this book, treats a similar encounter between a displaced old white Southerner and a young Northern black man. But by that time the civil rights movement had radically changed the South, and the confrontation between the old white man and the young black man also has a radically different outcome.

O'Connor's years at the Iowa Writers' Workshop saw her publish her first story in a national magazine and form friendships with other writers, most notably the talented but unstable poet Robert Lowell.

4

SOJOURN AT YADDO

IN 1947, THE POET ROBERT LOWELL visited Iowa and read at the Writers' Workshop. O'Connor met and was impressed by the young (30 years old) but prodigiously talented Lowell: he had recently won the Pulitzer Prize for his collection *Lord Weary's Castle.* She did not then realize how much better she would get to know Lowell—or that his incipient insanity, combined with her own fear of communism, would temporarily redirect her life in early 1949. But these events had not yet come to pass, and in 1947 O'Connor's mind was occupied primarily with completing her thesis at Iowa, which she had titled *The Geranium: A Collection of Short Stories,* and with trying to find college teaching jobs for the following fall. Accordingly, she submitted her thesis in June, but without a job in hand in September, she stayed on as a postgraduate student at the workshop. Meanwhile, she sold stories

O'Connor relaxes at the Yaddo artists' colony in upstate New York. The intricate wooden carvings and religious art were typical of the palatial colony, which was situated on the former estate of a wealthy, art-collecting couple, the Trasks.

to *Mademoiselle* and *Sewanee Review* and continued to work on *Wise Blood.*

In the spring of 1948, however, O'Connor received a prestigious invitation when the Yaddo Foundation asked her if she would like to spend June and July at its artists' colony near Saratoga Springs, New York. Flannery accepted, and in June she found herself at the palatial estate of the Trasks in upstate New York. Spencer Trask, a New York financier, and his wife, Katrina, had originally lived in the mansion that became the main building of Yaddo. Modeled on an English country house, the mansion also has touches of Gothic, Moorish, and Italian Renaissance architecture, and its furniture reflects its 19th-century eclectic style: expensive carpets cover the floors, carved wood and ecclesiastical furniture from Europe line the walls. Antiques abound inside the mansion; elaborate flower gardens and cultivated grounds thrive outside it.

Katrina Trask wished to turn Yaddo into a retreat for artists and writers, and after her husband died and she had married his friend, George Foster Peabody, her dream was accomplished. They opened the colony to visitors in 1926 and appointed Elizabeth Ames, an adopted relative of Mr. Peabody's, as director. Invitations to reside at Yaddo were, and are, based on creative productivity and recommendations; her new friend Robert Lowell, a frequent guest at the colony, and the recent successes of her stories no doubt helped Flannery to receive an invitation from Mrs. Ames. The colony was a perfect retreat for her: guests dined together in the mansion, but otherwise they spent their time in private cottages working. All expenses during the writers' residence were paid for by the Yaddo Foundation.

O'Connor therefore accepted her summer invitation with alacrity. In the meantime, Paul Engle of the Iowa Writers' Workshop offered her a modest fellowship at the workshop for the coming academic year. Ultimately, however, O'Connor turned down this offer—despite her mother's displeasure—because Elizabeth Ames had invited Flannery to return to Yaddo in mid-September and stay through the end of the academic year. After an August visit to her mother in Milledgeville, Flannery returned to the colony in September.

In the early fall, Flannery was one of 15 guests at the retreat, including Robert Lowell and the critic Malcolm Cowley. Both of them gave her advice on the crafting of *Wise Blood,* as well as other literary matters. During her sojourn at Yaddo, Flannery decided she was selling enough of her stories to need an agent to market them for her, and she hired Elizabeth McKee. McKee became a good friend and a frequent correspondent, in addition to placing Flannery's stories and novels with magazines and publishers.

Katrina Trask sits at her desk at the future site of Yaddo. Trask had long wanted to turn the estate into a retreat for artists and writers.

Early in 1949, however, Flannery's focus on her work was temporarily derailed by a controversy at Yaddo. Although an artists' "retreat," Yaddo could not escape from the world's politics, and some of the political upheaval following World War II had come into the colony with the artists themselves. The fear of communism in America, enflamed by Joseph Stalin's policies in the Soviet Union, had begun to intensify in the late 1940s. Senator Joseph McCarthy, whose name will forever be associated with the "Red Scare" of the 1950s, did not make his first big speech attacking Communists in the U.S. government until February 1950, but the groundwork for its reception had already been laid. America's writers were politicized either against Stalin and communism or—in fewer cases—for them. Everyone wore a political label of some kind, and paranoia had begun to infiltrate American culture, even extending into the idyllic estate outside Saratoga Springs.

Meanwhile, inside the luxurious compound of Yaddo, Robert Lowell was beginning to suffer the first cracks of a nervous breakdown. The critic Elizabeth Hardwick, who had moved to Yaddo during the winter and had a love affair with Lowell, noted that "he had the beginning of his breakdown there." Many of his other friends recognized that Lowell's letters to them had become strange and that he seemed "wound up" in January 1949. In February, the press gave him a focal point for what had come to be increasingly paranoid attitudes.

On February 11, 1949, an article in the *New York Times* accused a longtime Yaddo resident, Agnes Smedley, of being a Soviet spy. Smedley denied the charges, but Lowell and others were incensed at the possibility that a Communist had been welcomed at Yaddo. In fact, Smedley had enjoyed a long residence there—she had lived in one of the foundation's cottages, rent-free, from 1943 to March 1948. Most of the residencies were for a few months at best, and they were almost always reserved for creative

O'Connor, third from left, joins her fellow artists at Yaddo in a moment of merriment. During her sojourn at the colony, O'Connor received advice from the other writers on crafting her first novel.

writers. Smedley, however, wrote newspaper articles about Far East politics. Further, Smedley had been allowed other special privileges, including a private phone and her own personal taxi, while the other guests made do with the foundation's communal phone and vehicle.

On February 19, the U.S. Army denied the charges that had been leveled at Smedley—who had admitted to being a Communist but not a spy—but the damage had only begun among the guests at Yaddo. The FBI had appeared in the meantime and interviewed Elizabeth Hardwick and another guest, Edward Maisel. These two told Robert Lowell and Flannery O'Connor—the only other guests during February—what had transpired. Lowell became incensed. As his friend Robert Fitzgerald later described the poet's state of mind at this period, "the impression grew on Lowell that the outwardly benevolent institution had been given over to scandalous forces."

O'Connor, influenced by the powerful personality of Lowell and rather horrified by communism herself, agreed when he suggested that the writers in residence contact the board of directors of the foundation to complain. A meeting was convened in late February, and Lowell was chosen to speak for the writers. Lowell's speech was both eloquent and savage; he insisted that the director of Yaddo, Elizabeth Ames, be fired instantly from her post because "it is our impression that Mrs. Ames is somehow deeply and mysteriously involved in Mrs. Smedley's political activities." He then made an analogy likening Yaddo to a "body," and Mrs. Ames to "a diseased organ, chronically poisoning the whole system."

Lowell threatened the board further—if they did not immediately fire Mrs. Ames, he intended to tell all of his influential and famous writer friends to boycott Yaddo. He went on to name many of the most important writers of the 1940s, from Robert Frost and T. S. Eliot to W. H. Auden and John Berryman. Lowell's harangue went on for quite a long time and included his cross-examination of Elizabeth Hardwick and Flannery O'Connor, though all that they could say was that they had felt some unease during recent weeks at Yaddo.

Mrs. Ames defended herself by saying that Agnes Smedley had helped her to nurse her dying sister, and that she had therefore felt indebted to her and let her stay on at Yaddo in repayment. She also noted that until the newspaper report came out about Smedley, Lowell and O'Connor had seemed very happy at Yaddo. O'Connor, in fact, had asked to stay through July, and then to return the following year. Mrs. Ames described her guests before the news report:

> They frequently came to my house for music or cocktails, a harmonious life, with now and then little affectionate notes . . . then all of this changed with the morning of Tuesday, when they appeared at my door, looking extremely grave and upset. . . . I asked them, and they stated that the FBI had questioned them the day before. I was very much upset and disturbed . . . it was quite a shock to me to hear that.

The directors, refusing Lowell's demand that Ames be fired instantly, agreed to meet again in three weeks in New York to discuss the case at their regular meeting.

Robert Lowell and O'Connor tried to remove Elizabeth Ames, pictured below, from her position as director of the Yaddo colony because of her association with Agnes Smedley, an admitted Communist and longtime resident of Yaddo.

O'Connor wrote to Elizabeth McKee about the controversy on February 24.

> We have been very upset at Yaddo lately and all the guests are leaving in a group on Tuesday—the revolution. I'll probably have to be in New York for a month or so and I'll be looking for a place to stay. . . . All this is very disrupting to the book and has changed my plans entirely as I won't be coming back to Yaddo unless certain measures go into effect here.

The day after the meeting, Robert Lowell went to mass with Flannery and felt his Catholicism being revived. When he and Flannery visited the Fitzgeralds in New York shortly after that, Lowell told them that "he had returned to the Church that morning after receiving an incredible outpouring of grace."

As the Yaddo writers waited for the board of directors to reconvene, Flannery stayed in Elizabeth Hardwick's New York apartment, and Robert Lowell went to Rhode Island to spend a week in a Trappist monastery. Flannery admitted to friends that Lowell had worried her because he kept insisting she was a saint. Lowell's newfound interest in religion deepened and grew more fanatical. He called up the Fitzgeralds at 6:30 A.M. to tell them "Ash Wednesday was the day of the Word made Flesh," and then to detail how he had prayed in a bathtub of cold water to Flannery O'Connor's patron saint, St. Thérèse of Lisieux.

His friends began to worry about Lowell, while writers all over New York were discussing the second meeting of the Yaddo directors. Another group of Yaddo guests, who had seen the transcript of Lowell's harangue during the first directors' meeting, began to circulate a statement of support for Mrs. Ames. These writers declared, "we reject as preposterous the political charge being brought against Elizabeth Ames." They further documented their feelings:

> All of us have at one time or another, some of us for long periods, benefited from Elizabeth Ames's administration

In 1948, Robert Lowell puts a record on a phonograph in his Washington, D.C., office as the Capitol looms in the background. Lowell was an extremely gifted and influential poet, but he suffered from a number of nervous breakdowns.

of Yaddo. We are anti-Stalinists. We feel that the charge currently being brought arises from a frame of mind that represents a grave danger to both civil liberties and to the freedom necessary for the arts. We feel this charge involves a cynical assault not only on Elizabeth Ames's personal integrity, but also on the whole future of Yaddo.

These opponents of Robert Lowell's point of view regarding Mrs. Ames circulated 75 copies of this document and received 51 endorsements of Yaddo's director. Lowell was shocked and incredulous that his friends—for he knew these other writers, too—could have sided against him on the Ames issue.

When the Yaddo board remet on March 26, however, they agreed with Ames's supporters, and Lowell's and O'Connor's charges were dismissed. After this, Flannery took a room at the YWCA in New York City that she sardonically noted "smelled like an unopened Bible." She went back to work on *Wise Blood* with as much enthusiasm as she could muster, but the events at Yaddo had upset her, too. As Sally Fitzgerald put it,

> The episode left a deep impression on her, especially the unexpected and violent attack from the organized left, which I think did more to convince her of the possible justice of their charges than anything that had happened until then. . . . She lost no respect from anyone at Yaddo as a result of the episode. On the contrary, she was later cordially invited to return. The idea amused her.

Lowell, unfortunately, felt the deepest impact of the controversy, for it precipitated his complete mental breakdown. Soon after the second meeting that dismissed his charges, Lowell decided to go on a "missionary tour" of the Midwest, stopping first with Allen and Caroline Tate in Chicago. During his visit with the Tates, he began to have psychotic episodes. During one of these, he held Allen Tate at arm's length out of his second-floor apartment window and proceeded to recite one of Tate's most famous poems, "Ode to the Confederate Dead," to him. Tate was not amused, and told him to leave. Lowell went on to Bloomington, Indiana, to stay with the novelist Peter Taylor and his wife. But shortly after his arrival in Bloomington, Lowell stole a roll of tickets from a theater box office, and then beat up a policeman who tried to restrain him. He wound up in jail in Bloomington and then was moved by his family to a mental hospital outside of Georgetown, Massachusetts, where he began receiving electric shock treatment. When he was discharged from the hospital, and before he reentered another in New York, he married Elizabeth Hardwick.

Meanwhile, Allen Tate blamed Hardwick and O'Connor for setting Lowell off at Yaddo and for encouraging his crusade against Mrs. Ames. "But you are a woman and Miss O'Connor is a woman, and neither of you had the experience or knowledge to evaluate the situation in public terms," he concluded.

For her part, Flannery gave up the many advantages she had enjoyed at Yaddo—free room and board and time to work—in order to show her support for Robert Lowell. She did not go back to Saratoga Springs again, although she was invited, and she never blamed Lowell for her own collusion in "the communist scare." Instead, she lived in New York City until September 1949, although she disliked the place and her money was quickly running out.

Many of her short stories, such as "The Geranium," are about rural Southerners displaced in big cities. But in her typical witty fashion she told Betty Boyd Love that there was something to admire in New York City:

> There is one advantage in it because although you see several people you wish you didn't know, you see thousands you're glad you don't know.

Writer Katherine Anne Porter once said of O'Connor, "I am always astonished at Flannery's pictures which show nothing of her grace . . . she had a fine, clear, rosy skin and beautiful eyes."

5

A LIFELONG FRIENDSHIP

FLANNERY O'CONNOR first met Robert and Sally Fitzgerald in early March 1949. She had come down to New York City from Saratoga Springs with Elizabeth Hardwick and Robert Lowell, between the two hearings on the controversy at Yaddo. At the time, the Fitzgeralds were living with their two small children in an apartment on the East Side of Manhattan.

Both Robert and Sally were struck by their first meeting with the 24-year-old fiction writer from Milledgeville. She sat in a chair facing the windows, and the March light flickering off the East River illuminated her heart-shaped face. Robert noted that she looked "pale and glum, with fine eyes that could stop frowning and open brilliantly upon everything." Although she seemed shy, she was also clearly a young woman who knew her own mind. As Robert Lowell detailed the Yaddo controversy to the Fitzgeralds, Flannery struggled to bear him out

Sally Fitzgerald and five of her children pose on the lawn of their Connecticut home. O'Connor described Fitzgerald as "5 feet 2 inches tall and weighs at most 92 pounds except when she is pregnant which is most of the time."

without exaggerating what had happened at Saratoga Springs. The Fitzgeralds were impressed by her penetrating mind and sardonic wit, and they did not forget her.

In July 1949, when the impending birth of a third child led the Fitzgeralds to decide to move out of the city, they asked O'Connor if she would like to come and board with them in the Connecticut countryside. It was an ideal arrangement—O'Connor's shabby apartment on West 108th Street cost more than she could afford, and the Fitzgeralds needed the rent money a boarder could provide.

In September, O'Connor moved to the stone and timber house that the Fitzgeralds had purchased on a hilltop outside Ridgefield, Connecticut. Flannery settled into her own bedroom and bathroom over the garage. She had her own staircase and as much privacy as she wanted, but the living conditions were austere. The room's furniture consisted of little more than a bed, a desk, and a Sears-Roebuck dresser that Sally and Robert had painted bright blue. The walls were constructed of beaverboard, which did little to keep out the Connecticut winter. Nor did they keep out the field mice, which O'Connor could hear skittering between the beaverboard and the timber. She pushed pins through the boards and told the Fitzgeralds that maybe if the mice hurt their feet, they would decamp. As the winter winds whipped the house, O'Connor and the Fitzgeralds stuffed their window cracks with pages from the *New York Times.*

Nevertheless, despite the chill, the three adults and two children lived contentedly in the house nestled in the oak and laurel forest. The adults had much in common, for they all loved literature. O'Connor was at work on *Wise Blood,* and Robert had recently translated the Greek classics *Oedipus Rex* and *Oedipus at Colonus.* Sally regularly reviewed books for a number of periodicals. At night, after the children were in bed, Flannery, Robert, and Sally would sit in the living room with a pitcher of martinis and talk about books and writing and their lives. As Robert later recalled, "Our talks then and at the dinner table were long and lighthearted, and they were our movies, our concerts, and our theatre."

The days, like the evenings, followed a pleasant regular pattern. O'Connor attended mass every morning in the nearby village of Georgetown, and the Fitzgeralds took turns driving her there. (One parent always stayed home to watch the babies and start breakfast.) After mass they had breakfast together, and then O'Connor disappeared to her study-bedroom to work. She wrote for four hours every morning. At noon she would reappear in jeans and a sweater and stroll a half-mile down the hill to the mailbox. Even then, her correspondence was considerable; later in life, when lupus confined her to the Milledgeville farm, almost all of her important relationships would be carried on through letters.

During this time Robert Fitzgerald taught classics at Sarah Lawrence College, about an hour's drive from the Ridgefield house. That year he taught his students Dante's *Divine Comedy,* and everyone in the house read it. O'Connor loaned him Faulkner's *As I Lay Dying,* a book she felt had greatly influenced her own writing. But Fitzgerald's recent translation of Sophocles's *Oedipus Rex* and *Oedipus at Colonus* had also influenced her. At a moment of uncertainty over the best way to finish off Hazel Motes's life in *Wise Blood,* she read the Oedipus plays. After that, she knew how to end her book: Hazel, like Oedipus, blinds himself. She then reworked the whole of *Wise Blood* to prepare for the new ending.

Years later, Robert Fitzgerald nostalgically remembered the year O'Connor spent in Connecticut.

A scene from John Huston's movie version of Wise Blood *shows Hazel (right) talking to a preacher who has supposedly blinded himself with lime. Although the preacher has actually just scarred his face, Hazel does blind himself with lime, a plot twist inspired by* Oedipus Rex.

So that year passed in our wilderness. The leaves turned, the rains came, the woods were bared, the snows fell and glittered, fenders were belted by broken chains, the winter stars shone out. In the early mornings we had the liturgies of All Hallows, All Souls, Advent, Christmas, Epiphany. The diaper truck and the milk truck slogged in and slogged out. We worked on at our jobs through thaws and buds, through the May flies, and into summer, when we could take our evening ease in deckchairs on the grass.

In May, the Fitzgeralds had another child, and O'Connor became its godmother. She had become one of the family, taking a child for a walk or up to her room to play. She told the Fitzgeralds that she was sure the kids referred to the three of them as "he," "she," and "the other one."

Their idyllic life together continued into a second fall, until December when Flannery began to complain of pain in her upper arms. She went to see a local doctor who suspected rheumatoid arthritis, but he told her to double-check it at a hospital in Milledgeville. Flannery left early for Christmas in Georgia, becoming desperately ill on the train home. She spent most of the spring in the hospital, too sick to write the Fitzgeralds until that summer; meanwhile, her mother kept them up-to-date on Flannery's health. During this time Flannery still intended to return to Connecticut when her health improved. She wrote her friends on September 20, 1951,

> I reckon you all are underway with the academic yer [year] '51–'52 and No. 5. I hope this one will be a girl & have a fierce Old Testament name and cut off a lot of heads. You had better stay down and take care of yourself. Your children sound big enough to do all the work. By beating them moderately and moderately often you should be able to get them in the habit of doing domestic chores. . . . I have twenty-one brown ducks with blue wing bars. They walk everywhere they go in single-file.

As the Fitzgeralds continued to have children and enjoy their health, Flannery had only her birds, her daily battles

Roadside signs and other public displays were often used to spread Christianity in the South, which meant that a person with no formal training could still get a rigorous religious education. O'Connor often wrote about characters who, as she put it, were practicing a "natural" religion, with no authoritative leader or church to aid them in constructing their religious life.

with lupus, and her fiction. Nevertheless, no hint of despair at her own limited life ever escaped from her—at least, not in her letters.

In June 1952, O'Connor returned to visit the Fitzgeralds in Ridgefield. Robert Fitzgerald remembers that she looked "ravaged but pretty, with short soft new curls." Sally fed her watercress and herbs because Flannery still maintained a salt-free diet. Unfortunately, though they were delighted to reunite, Flannery and the Fitzgeralds could not recreate the idyllic year they had spent when she was their boarder. One reason was the presence of two new members of the household. One of these was a displaced person from Yugoslavia (after World War II, many American families took in displaced people, or "D.P.'s," whose homes had been destroyed by fighting); the other was a 12-year-old black girl from Harlem in New York City. The D.P., Maria Ivancic, took an instant dislike to Loretta, the black girl, whom the Fitzgeralds had invited up through the Fresh Air Fund. Sally Fitzgerald, who was then pregnant with her fifth child, remembers:

> Maria was instantly allergic to our guest (she had never seen a black before) and began to behave very badly, afflicting us all with scowls, mutterings, and tantrums of varying intensity, in Slovenian. After a few days of this, I was threatened with a miscarriage; and Flannery came down with a virus, which of course alarmed us all.

Robert Fitzgerald could not help out because he had gone to Indiana for six weeks to teach at the Indiana School of Letters. When he returned, Flannery had already gone home sick to Milledgeville, with Loretta in tow as far as New York City. She wrote him in July to describe the final scenes with Loretta and Maria.

> I hated to leave Sally there with only Maria when she was sick, but as I seemed to be getting sick myself, I thought I had better. Also, I was able to take M. Loretta back to New York with me and leave her in the lap of the welfare woman. I felt that when she was gone, Sally would be better. Loretta would perhaps have been controllable if there had been a Federal Marshal in the house.

It is interesting that Flannery blames Loretta's "wise sass and argument" (same letter) for most of the household's troubles that June while Sally Fitzgerald blames Maria's racism. After reading the above letter to Robert, Sally claimed that the comment about Loretta's needing a federal marshal was "pure Georgia rhetoric on Flannery's part, Loretta having been too shy during her visit to do anything but stand around caressing the blond heads of our young."

O'Connor continued to write the Fitzgeralds regularly from Andalusia, letting them know the progress of her work. In December 1952, she wrote to tell them that she had won a Kenyon Fellowship: $2,000 from the *Kenyon Review,* a top-notch literary magazine located at Kenyon College in Gambier, Ohio.

> I reckon most of this money will go to blood and ACTH [cortisone] and books, with a few sideline researches into the ways of the vulgar. I would like to go to California for about two minutes to further these researches, though at times I feel that a feeling for the vulgar is my natural talent and don't need any particular encouragement. Did you see the picture of Roy Rogers's horse attending a church service in Pasadena? I forgot whether his name was Tex or Trigger but he was dressed fit to kill and looked like he was having a good time.

Flannery enjoyed sending them the news from Milledgeville and any newspaper clippings that she thought particularly amusing. The Fitzgeralds sent her books and other gifts they thought she could use. O'Connor responded enthusiastically to a new salt-free cereal they had found for her.

> The Maple Oats really send me. I mean they are a heap of improvement over saltless oatmeal, horse biscuit, stewed Kleenex, and the other delicacies that I have been eating. They send Regina too but I think it is because they smell like what the cows here eat.

The same letter also reveals that Flannery's mother, Regina, apparently did not share her daughter's enthusiasm for literature.

> My mamma and I have interesting literary discussions like the following which took place over some Modern Library books that I had just ordered:
>
> SHE: "*Mobby Dick.* I've always heard about that."
> ME: "*Mow-by Dick.*"

In 1949, the year O'Connor boarded at the Fitzgeralds', Robert Fitzgerald holds his eldest daughter at their Ridgefield, Connecticut, home.

SHE: "*Mow-by Dick. The Idiot.* You would get something called *Idiot.* What's it about?"
ME: "An Idiot."

In October 1953, the Fitzgeralds moved to Siena, Italy. Robert had just received an advance to write an English translation of *The Odyssey* for Doubleday. O'Connor visited them in late August for the last time before they left the United States. This visit went far better than the last, and she stayed for three weeks despite her mother's injunctions to only stay one and not "overdo" her health.

In the years that followed, O'Connor wrote many of her wittiest and warmest letters to the Fitzgeralds, who continued to live in Italy. In 1955, she dedicated her second book, the collection of short stories entitled *A Good Man Is Hard to Find* to "Sally and Robert Fitzgerald." In 1957, she saw Robert again in South Bend, Indiana, where he had invited her to give a lecture at the University of Notre Dame (he was a visiting professor there at the time). Two hundred and fifty people came to her talk, which was about the grotesque in Southern fiction. Robert noted that she seemed "frail but steady, no longer disfigured by any swelling, and her hair had grown long again." He also took note of her crutches, which had become permanent additions to her wardrobe as her hips deteriorated under the onslaught of her illness.

In 1958, O'Connor would see the entire Fitzgerald family again for the first time in five years. She and her mother met them in Italy during a European trip given her

This photo, taken in 1952 for the jacket of Wise Blood, *shows O'Connor after her first bout of lupus. It became clear to O'Connor that her health would not allow her to travel and stay with friends like the Fitzgeralds; however, she maintained her friendship with them and many others through letters.*

by Katie Semmes, her wealthy Savannah cousin. After a few days with the Fitzgeralds in the seaside town of Liguria, O'Connor went on to "take the cure" in the waters of Lourdes, France, and Sally Fitzgerald accompanied her.

Robert Fitzgerald remembers seeing her only two more times: once in April 1961 when he visited Andalusia, and then at the Smith College commencement in 1963 when O'Connor received an honorary degree. By early 1964, however, her health began its steady decline, and she never saw the Fitzgeralds again.

In a life filled with literary friendships, perhaps the most enduring and rewarding for O'Connor was the one she shared with the Fitzgeralds. After living with them in Connecticut, she called them her "adopted kinfolks," and she never lost her interest in their lives and their activities. For their part, they have been the greatest champions of Flannery O'Connor's literary reputation. Robert Fitzgerald's memoir of Flannery in the introduction to *Everything That Rises Must Converge* is the best source of biographical information currently available on O'Connor. He and Sally Fitzgerald have been her literary executors, providing detailed introductions to O'Connor's novels and short-story collections. Sally Fitzgerald has also edited O'Connor's collected letters, *The Habit of Being* (1979), and provided a meticulous chronology of Flannery's short life in the 1988 *Collected Works,* published by the Library of America.

Sally Fitzgerald described the quality of O'Connor's friendship in *The Habit of Being:*

> Flannery was a likable young woman, and she had many friends. [Her letters] show her willing involvement in the lives of her friends, and the welcome she gave them into her own. She wrote to her closest correspondent that she needed people. Her letters suggest that many of those with whom she came in contact came to realize that they needed her as well.

The dust jacket of the 1955 hardcover British edition of Wise Blood *shows a pious Hazel praying in front of his car. Presumably, O'Connor liked this jacket better than that of a paperback edition of the novel where, she complained, one of her female characters "is thereon turned into Marilyn Monroe in underclothes."*

6

DISPLACED PERSONS

IN 1953, FLANNERY O'CONNOR was permanently ensconced at Andalusia, working steadily on a new collection of short stories and observing life on her mother's farm. In January, Regina O'Connor searched the county for new hired help to manage the dairy, an enterprise that Flannery watched with great amusement. A letter to the Fitzgeralds in late January describes some of the "good country people" that Regina had been considering for the job after letting go of "the J——s" in 1952. (Full names were occasionally omitted from O'Connor's published letters out of respect for the subjects' privacy.)

[Regina] has been dickering with the C——B——s to take the J——s place. Old man J—— looked like he might have had an ancestor back a couple of centuries who was at least a decayed gentleman (he wouldn't wear overalls; only khaki) but these C——B——s look like they've been joined up with the human race for only a couple of months now. Mrs. B—— says she went to school for one day and didn't loin nothin

and ain't went back. She has four children and I thought
she was one of them. The oldest girl is 14 with a mouth
full of snuff. The first time I saw her she had long yellow
hair and the next time it was short in an all-over good-for-
life permanent and Regina says—they were standing outside the car and we were in—"I see you have a new
permanent." "Got it Sad-day," she says and then another
pair of hands and eyes pulls up on the window of the car
and says "I'm gonter git me mine next Sad-day." Mamma
has one too.

O'Connor describes the C——B——s for the Fitzgeralds
with the eye and ear of a master fiction writer. She shows
what they value (hairdos) and what they do not (education)
from their conversation, while also revealing what they
look like and what level of society they are from. Such
closely observed and carefully rendered characters distinguish all of O'Connor's short stories. In the tales written
during these first years at Andalusia, later collected as *A
Good Man Is Hard to Find,* fictional characters modeled
on people like the "J——s" and the "C——B——'s"
appear often.

O'Connor had accepted the limitations of her lupus,
coming to see the illness as a kind of blessing in disguise:
it had brought her home and forced her to write about
what she knew best, her own region and people. In March
1953, she wrote a stoical letter about her condition to the
Lowells.

> My father had [lupus] some twelve or fifteen years ago but
> at that time there was nothing for it but the undertaker;
> now it can be controlled with the ACTH. I have enough
> energy to write with and as that is all I have any business
> doing anyhow, I can with one eye squinted take it all as a
> blessing. What you have to measure out, you come to
> observe closer or so I tell myself.

After this burst of serious candor, Flannery closed the
letter in her usual joking tone:

My mother and I live on a large place and I have bought me some peafowl and sit on the back steps a good deal studying them. I am going to be the World Authority on Peafowl, and I hope to be offered a chair some day at the Chicken College.

By early 1954 Flannery's hips had also begun to disintegrate, and she observed to a friend, "I am not able enough to walk straight but not crippled enough to walk with a cane so that I give the appearance of merely being a little drunk all the time."

Flannery, whose limp had "displaced" her center of gravity, and whose lupus had re-placed her in her native South, must have felt a particular affinity for people adapting to new situations and places. "The Displaced Person,"

Male and female scarecrows watch over two white women working a garden. Poor whites in the South, like Mrs. Shortley in "The Displaced Person," were only marginally better-off than poor blacks and jealously guarded what position and prestige they did have in society.

one of the earliest stories written for *A Good Man Is Hard to Find,* came from her observations of farm life. Her mother managed several sets of employees, from the two regular black workers (Shot and Louis) to the white hired help who ran the dairy to a succession of Eastern European families—D.P.'s—who came to live with her in the years after World War II. The clashes of these different classes and their different backgrounds, races, and expectations appear in several of O'Connor's stories, but most poignantly in "The Displaced Person."

This story is the longest in the collection, and one of the most famous of all her tales. The main characters are Mrs. McIntyre, a sixtyish widow who is managing a dairy farm on her own; Mr. and Mrs. Shortley, the white hired help who run the dairy; the Guizacs, a displaced family from Poland recently hired by Mrs. McIntyre; an old priest; and the two black laborers, Astor (an old man) and Sulk, a light-colored young man. The plot of the story is spun from Mrs. Shortley's fear that the Guizacs—who are highly industrious and efficient—will replace her and Mr. Shortley on the farm. Mrs. Shortley's fears are well grounded on the fact that Mrs. McIntyre praises Mr. Guizac's hard work and implies that the Shortleys do not save her any money. (Mrs. McIntyre's primary character trait is an obsession with making and saving money.)

Finally, in a rage, the Shortleys leave the farm and Mrs. McIntyre is left to cope with the Guizacs, but her departed dairy workers have made her suspicious of them. The culminating conflict of the story occurs when Mrs. McIntyre discovers that Mr. Guizac has offered to let Sulk, the young black man, marry Guizac's white cousin so that she can get out of a D.P. camp in Europe and live in America. Despite all of Mr. Guizac's industry, Mrs. McIntyre is horrified by the idea that he would permit his white cousin to marry a black man; her horror reflects that of most middle-class white Southerners from the 1700s to the late 1900s, and it blinds her to Mr. Guizac's excellent working abilities. She decides to get rid of the displaced people, despite her agreement with the priest.

In the last scenes of the story, Mrs. McIntyre has rehired Mr. Shortley and determined to fire Mr. Guizac, although what she feels as a moral obligation to the priest keeps her from doing so immediately. In the disturbing climax of the story, Mrs. McIntyre, with the silent collusion of Astor and Mr. Shortley, permits Mr. Guizac to be killed by a tractor. As the parked tractor starts to roll down a hill toward Guizac, none of the others call out to warn him. This evil accident results in the departure of Sulk and Mr. Shortley and in Mrs. McIntyre's financial and physical ruin.

Flannery's reflections on the relationship between the various classes of white and black Southerners, combined with the added complication of a family of displaced persons, probably came from her own experiences at Andalusia. Late in 1951, Regina invited the O'Connors' first family of European refugees to live on the farm, an act that immediately aroused the fear of one "Mrs. P.," the current dairyman's wife. An excerpt from a letter written to Sally and Robert Fitzgerald in December 1951 reveals that Mrs. P.'s personality strongly resembles that of Mrs. Shortley in "The Displaced Person."

> My mamma is getting ready for what she hopes will be one of her blessings: a refugee family to arrive here Christmas night. . . . She and Mrs. P., the dairyman's wife, have been making curtains for the windows out of flowered chicken-feed sacks. Regina was complaining that the green sacks wouldn't look so good in the same room where the pink ones were and Mrs. P. (who has no teeth on one side of her mouth) says in a very superior voice, "Do you think they'll know what colors even is?"

Mrs. P.'s ignorance about the Poles is echoed by Mrs. Shortley's in "The Displaced Person." In the story, Mrs. Shortley is the character who explains the arrival of the Guizacs to the two black workers. Astor asks her:

> "Who they now?"
>
> "They come from over the water," Mrs. Shortley said with a wave of her arm. "They're what is called Displaced Persons."
>
> "Displaced Persons," he said. "Well now. I declare. What do that mean?"
>
> "It means they ain't where they were born at and there's nowhere for them to go—like if you was run out of here and wouldn't nobody have you."
>
> "It seem like they here, though," the old man said in a reflective voice. "If they here, they somewhere." . . .
>
> The illogic of Negro-thinking always irked Mrs. Shortley. "They ain't where they belong to be at," she said. "They belong to be back over yonder where everything is still like they been used to. Over here it's more advanced than where they come from. But yawl better look out now," she said and nodded her head. "There's about ten million billion more just like them."

This passage reveals that Mrs. Shortley is both a racist and a troublemaker. She hopes to make the black workers afraid that they will lose their jobs to the Guizacs, when it is really her own and Mr. Shortley's jobs that are threatened.

However, Regina's Polish family did not turn out to be as industrious as the fictional Guizacs. Two years after their arrival O'Connor commented on them again to Robert and Sally Fitzgerald: "My mama is thinking about getting a Hungarian family. We still have the Poles but they are mighty trying and trifling at this point. She will not let them go but they do very little. The question will be how many mixtures can you add to the broth without its exploding."

In "The Displaced Person," the broth explodes. The D.P.'s displace both the black workers and the Shortleys as Mrs. McIntyre's most industrious employees. "Mr. Guizac could drive a tractor, use the rotary hay-baler, the silage cutter, the combine, the letz mill, or any other machine she had on the place. He was an expert mechanic, a carpenter, and a mason. He was thrifty and energetic." The Shortleys hardly measure up, and Mrs. McIntyre enjoys letting them know it.

> "At last," she said, "I've got somebody I can depend on. For years I've been fooling with sorry people. Sorry people. Poor white trash and niggers," she muttered. "They've drained me dry."

But O'Connor's story treats more than the class upheaval caused by the last addition to "the broth." She also explores the quintessential "sin" of the South: miscegenation (the intermarriage of whites and blacks). This fear among white Southerners is reflected in Mrs. McIntyre, who is appalled when she discovers that Mr. Guizac intends to marry his cousin to Sulk. When she confronts Mr. Guizac on this issue, her words could have been taken directly from almost any of the white politicians holding office in Georgia in the 1940s and 1950s.

> Monster! she said to herself and looked at him as if she were seeing him for the first time. . . . "Mr. Guizac," she said, beginning slowly and then speaking fast until she ended breathless in the middle of a word, "that nigger cannot have a white wife from Europe. You can't talk to a nigger that way. You'll excite him and besides it can't be done. Maybe it can be done in Poland but it can't be done here and you'll have to stop. It's all foolishness."

Mr. Guizac, whose cousin has been in a refugee camp for three years, does not care that Sulk is black, but Mrs. McIntyre is outraged, and she is determined to get rid of anyone who might upset the power balance of white superiority and black inferiority.

Nevertheless she is afraid of the priest, who represents Christian charity in this story. He tells her not to turn the Guizacs out, to "think of the thousands of them, think of the ovens and the boxcars and the camps and the sick children and Christ Our Lord." But Mrs. McIntyre cannot open her mind to any of that; she replies, "He's extra and he's upset the balance around here." Her lack of charity toward the displaced person causes the eventual downfall of the farm, and all balance is lost forever. Mrs. McIntyre's farm collapses due to an act of racism; a fate, O'Connor seems to hint, that awaits the South if white Southerners continue to treat black Southerners as second-class citizens.

There are several references to Christ in the story, some of which subtly encourage comparisons between Guizac and Jesus. When Mrs. McIntyre complains to the priest about Guizac, saying, "He didn't have to come in the first place," he answers, "He came to redeem us." Later Mrs. McIntyre says, "As far as I'm concerned, Christ was just another D.P." The deep significance of her remark is lost on Mrs. McIntyre, an irony typical of an O'Connor story. But O'Connor is not implying a simple one-to-one correlation between Guizac and Christ; though her stories can almost be read as parables, meanings are never reducible to a single interpretation. They always open out into disturbingly complex, occasionally paradoxical examinations of profound issues.

Another story in the same collection, "The Artificial Nigger," also treats the theme of racism, although in this one she restricts the conflict to blacks and whites rather than "displacing" it onto foreign visitors. Briefly, "The Artificial Nigger" follows an old white man, Mr. Head, and his grandson Nelson as they spend a day in Atlanta. Mr. Head wants to show Nelson that the city is an evil place, nowhere worth living compared to their life in the country. He describes the city's sewer system as a descent into hell, and he makes them walk in circles around the city to avoid getting lost. Soon, however, they turn into a black neighborhood, where they do get lost. Both grandfather and grandson grow fearful of the "black eyes in black faces" that watch them—the only whites on the street. When Nelson accidentally knocks down a pedestrian and bystanders call for the police, Mr. Head denies knowing him and walks away. Nelson follows him, his shock replaced by rage, and Mr. Head feels a sense of despair at having denied his own grandson. They are both saved, however, when they come upon a statue of an "artificial nigger" (a ceramic figure, usually found in a garden, of a black jockey holding a brass ring), a symbol that reunites them "like an act of mercy."

O'Connor commented later to "A.," the young woman who became one of her most important correspondents, that "The Artificial Nigger" was her favorite story. "There is nothing that screams out the tragedy of the South like what my uncle calls 'nigger statuary.' And then there's Peter's denial [of Jesus]. They all got together in that one." To another friend she explained the story even more explicitly: "What I had in mind to suggest with the artificial nigger was the redemptive quality of the Negro's suffering for us all."

However tragic O'Connor's stories are, they never sink into mere melodrama and sentimentality. One of her great gifts is to leaven tragedy with humor; her humor keeps people reading, while her sense of tragedy keeps them thinking about the stories long after they have finished. She wrote to A. in September 1955: "The Comic and the Terrible . . . may be opposite sides of the same coin. In my own experience, everything funny I have written is more terrible than it is funny, or only funny because it is terrible, or only terrible because it is funny." She confided to another correspondent how much the stories in *A Good Man Is Hard to Find* pleased her. "The truth is, I like them better than anybody and I read them over and over and laugh and laugh, then get embarrassed when I remember I was the one wrote them."

In June 1955, *A Good Man Is Hard to Find* came out to great critical acclaim. Although there were some negative reviews, for the most part this collection of stories received

A broken-down statue of a black jockey deteriorates in a field. O'Connor maintained "there is nothing that screams out the tragedy of the South like what my uncle calls 'nigger statuary.'"

Gene Kelly plays Mr. Shiftlet in the television dramatization of "The Life You Save May Be Your Own." O'Connor felt that Kelly was far too genial for the role; however, he was not exactly miscast because the network rewrote the story so that Mr. Shiftlet honorably returns to his wife in the end.

high praise—far higher than that accorded to *Wise Blood* a few years before. Harvey Breit of NBC-TV invited her to appear on his show for an interview and to see a dramatization of the opening scene of another one of the stories, "The Life You Save May Be Your Own." Although O'Connor consented to the interview, she felt awkward about it and told a friend, "I will probably not be able to think of anything to say to Mr. Harvey Breit but 'Huh?' and 'Ah dunno.' When I come back I'll probably have to spend three months day and night in the chicken pen to counteract these evil influences."

She predicted that "as no New Yorker has any insight into what comes out of the South, I know it will be a mess—actors without shoes, New Jersey hillbilly voices, etc., etc. And then I have a mental picture of my glacial glare being sent out over the nation onto millions of children who are impatiently waiting for The Batman to come on." As it happened, however, she later described the event as only "mildly ghastly," and it did help the sales of the new book.

Meanwhile, O'Connor augmented her income by giving talks to women's groups and colleges around the nation. Her talks to aspiring literary women gave O'Connor a good deal of funny material, which she put in her letters to friends, such as the excerpt below to A.

> The jamboree in Athens [Georgia] was a real farce. Penwomen! Nothing but penwomen and believe me they are a tribe apart; they are mostly over sixty, blood-thirsty to sell, they will take any amount of encouragement and their works are heavily inspirational.

Mostly, however, these talks tired and annoyed O'Connor. In another letter to A. she commented, "I always come away with a lot of faces without names and a lot of names without faces and it is very frustrating."

These trips became more difficult because Flannery's hips had further disintegrated. By the end of 1954 she was forced to walk with a cane. By 1955 she had to use crutches, which she hated, for she found them both awkward and humiliating. She expressed her feelings in the following letter to A.:

> I have decided I must be a pretty pathetic sight with these crutches. I was in Atlanta the other day in Davisons. An old lady got on the elevator behind me and as soon as I turned around she fixed me with a moist gleaming eye and said in a loud voice, "Bless you, darling!" . . . I gave her a weakly lethal look, whereupon greatly encouraged, she grabbed my arm and whispered (very loud) in my ear, "Remember what they said to John at the gate, darling!" It was not my floor but I got off and I suppose the old lady was astounded at how quick I could get away on crutches.

> I have a one-legged friend and I asked her what they said
> to John at the gate. She said she reckoned they said, "The
> lame shall enter first." This may be because the lame will
> be able to knock everybody else aside with their crutches.

In her last collection of stories, *Everything That Rises Must Converge,* O'Connor included a story entitled "The Lame Shall Enter First" about a juvenile delinquent with a club-foot. No doubt the idea for the story was intimately connected with her own worsening lameness, a state that often made her both angry and embarrassed.

In 1956, after the success of the partial dramatization of "The Life You Save May Be Your Own," the General Electric Playhouse approached Flannery about making a television show of the entire story. Flannery sold the television rights to the story and bought her mother a refrigerator with the money. She wrote to A., "While they make hash out of my story, she and me will make ice in the new refrigerator."

"The Life You Save May Be Your Own" is another of Flannery's most popular stories. It is about a con man, Mr. Shiftlet, who appears on a poor Southern farm looking for work. Only two people live on the farm, an old woman named Mrs. Crater and her retarded daughter, Lucynell. Shiftlet wants two things from Mrs. Crater: an old car she keeps in a garage and as much of her money as he can get. To attain these goals he marries Lucynell and drives off with her on their "honeymoon." When she falls asleep in a diner at the end of their first day, he leaves her and flees back to his hometown of Mobile, Alabama. Mr. Shiftlet's character is that of "a devil in disguise," and O'Connor's stories and novels contain many such figures.

For the TV episode of this story, the producers (Ronald Reagan among them) chose the dancer Gene Kelly for the role of Shiftlet. Flannery was horrified as well as amused. "I am writing my agent to make haste and sell all my stories for musical comedies. There ought to be enough tap dancers around to take care of them, and there's always Elvis

Presley." The TV show appeared in February 1957, and Flannery pronounced it "slop of the third water," although it made her even more famous in Milledgeville. The college librarian had a dinner party to which she invited Flannery, Regina, and six of the local old ladies.

> All the old ladies were entranced. They thought it was the sweetest thing they had ever seen. All over town old ladies were gathered to witness it. And other groups too. . . . My mother has been collecting congratulations all week like eggs in a basket. Several children have stopped me on the street and complimented me. Dogs who live in houses with television have paused to sniff me. The local city fathers think I am a credit now to the community. One old lady said, "That was a play that really made me think!" I didn't ask her what. As for me, I stood the play a good deal better than I am standing the congratulations.

When the hubbub from the success of the television show died down, Flannery returned quietly to work on her second novel, *The Violent Bear It Away.*

As 1957 drew to a close and her health continued to worsen, her 88-year-old Savannah cousin, Katie Semmes, offered to send Flannery and her mother on a trip to Lourdes, France. Cousin Katie hoped that the supposedly blessed water there might cure Flannery's lupus. Despite her dislike of long-distance travel and her reluctance to bathe in the curative waters, Flannery agreed at last to take the trip to Europe.

In 1961, O'Connor relaxes on the porch of the Cline House. By this time she was one of the most prominent regional writers in the United States and was a popular lecturer on Southern literature.

7

A BRAVE SPIRIT

O'CONNOR AGREED TO ACCEPT her cousin's gift of a pilgrimage to Lourdes when she realized that she would be able to see the Fitzgeralds in Europe—they were still living in Italy at that time. Accordingly, she wrote to them in November 1957:

> My mother is all for [the trip]. I think I may be able to stand it if I just cut my motor off and allow myself to be towed behind the old lady. . . . I don't know whether I am expected to wash my bones in the waters of Lourds or not; that don't interest me in the least; I think the crutches preferable to having to do it. . . . Be prepared to visit the dowdy pilgrums in Rome. I'll probably need artificial respiration by that time.

In early February, however, the trip was briefly called off. Flannery wrote Maryat Lee to say that the doctor said she could not go because of her lupus. Nevertheless, she showed her characteristic sense of good humor by praising the cortisone that kept her alive at all, even if it could not make her well enough to travel.

> I owe my existence and cheerful countenance to the pituitary glands of thousands of pigs butchered daily in Chicago Illinois at the Armour packing plant. If pigs wore garments I wouldn't be worthy to kiss the hems of them.

Later that month the doctor changed his mind, and O'Connor wrote the Fitzgeralds again to implore them to meet her and her mother in Milan, Italy. "Left for two minutes alone in foreign parts," she worried, "Regina and I would probably end up behind the Iron Curtain asking the way to Lourdes in sign language. I cannot bear to contemplate it."

As their preparations for the trip continued, O'Connor worked daily on her new novel, enjoyed her Andalusia aviary, and wrote letters to her friends. Her correspondence with A. focused more and more on the religious aspects of her fiction. In her responses to this correspondent, O'Connor began to describe in detail how her own deep Catholicism influenced her writing. "It seems to me that all good stories are about conversion," she explained to A., "about a character's changing. . . . The action of grace changes a character." She further argued, "All my stories are about the action of grace on a character who is not very willing to support it, but most people think of these stories as hard, hopeless, brutal, etc."

During this time O'Connor was attempting to describe the action of grace on Francis Marion Tarwater, the hero of her novel, while she continued to read the work of other writers—novelists, philosophers, and theologians. In late March 1958, Flannery met another important Southern writer, Katherine Anne Porter. Porter had given a reading in Macon after which mutual friends, the Gossetts, brought her to Andalusia. Porter told Flannery that she had always wanted to go to Lourdes, to pray that she might finish the novel she had been working on for 27 years (*The Ship of*

Fools). Flannery thought her a charming old woman of 65, "very pleasant and agreeable, crazy about my peacocks; plowed all over the yard behind me in her spike-heeled shoes to see my various kinds of chickens."

At last April 22 arrived and Regina and Flannery left for Europe. Flannery caught a cold early in the trip and felt ill for almost all of it. She wrote to the poet Elizabeth Bishop that "my capacity for staying at home has now been perfected, sealed & is going to last me the rest of my life." Lourdes, she found "was not as bad as I expected it to be. It is a beautiful village or would be if it weren't pockmarked with religious junk shops." Despite her earlier determination not to bathe, Flannery did take a dip in the holy water and also drank some of it from a Thermos bottle passed among the visitors. "I had a nasty cold," she confessed, "so I figured I left more germs than I took away." The best part of the trip for Flannery was getting to see the Fitzgeralds—Sally accompanied her to Lourdes—and meeting the pope. She described the pope as "very much alive. Never seen anybody quite so alive."

In June 1958, glad to be back home, Flannery decided to learn to drive a car and began to take lessons. Her first efforts were unsuccessful, however. "To prove that I ain't adjusted to the modern world, I failed the driving test. Now in two weeks I have to go take it again. I barely brought the patrolman back alive so I don't know if he'll relish taking me around the block again." Eventually she passed the test, but she never learned to like driving, so Regina continued to be the preferred chauffeur.

Work on her second novel, *The Violent Bear It Away,* was going well, and in a few months she wrote to A.,

> I am very near the end of my opus. Three or four more pages and I'll have a first draft. This is a very good feeling I can tell you after so many years. Of course now I have to go back to the beginning. I'm by no means finished but at least I know it's possible. I must say I attribute this to Lourdes.

The Violent Bear It Away resembles her first novel, *Wise Blood*, in that Francis Marion Tarwater, the young hero of *The Violent Bear It Away,* feels fated to preach in the same way that Hazel Motes did in the first novel. Both characters fight against this sense of predestination; both of them are transformed and redeemed by moments of violence.

The Violent Bear It Away begins with the death of Francis's great-uncle, Mason Tarwater. Mason has raised Francis Tarwater to be a prophet, "to expect the Lord's call himself," but Tarwater wants heartily to reject this fate. The conflict in the story comes through Tarwater's uncle, Rayber, a schoolteacher who lives in the city. Mason had attempted to make Rayber a prophet before Tarwater, but Rayber had rejected these teachings and had become an intellectual instead. After the death of the old man, Rayber hopes to turn Tarwater from religious faith to nonreligious reason. Young Tarwater is not attracted to Rayber's beliefs, either, but he is attracted—and repelled—by Rayber's retarded son, Bishop. Tarwater has a revelation about Bishop in which he realizes that his first act as a prophet must be to baptize the dim-witted boy.

In the second part of the book, Tarwater is living in the city with his uncle Rayber. The city is the same lonely, dangerous place that O'Connor describes in all of her stories about urban life. Then the scene shifts, and Rayber takes Tarwater and Bishop to Cherokee Lodge, a place in the countryside. On this excursion Tarwater attempts to come to peace with Rayber, but he also baptizes—and drowns—Bishop. During this part of the novel, Tarwater is plagued by the Devil in several disguises, ranging from a "Friend" who talks inside his head to an old-looking young man who gives him a ride in a lavender-and-cream-colored car and then rapes him in the woods.

After this act of violence, Tarwater accepts his destiny as a prophet. He sets the woods on fire around his childhood home—the farm of the dead Mason Tarwater—and

He knew that his destiny forced him on to a final revelation. His scorched eyes no longer looked hollow or as if
they were meant only to guide him forward. They looked
as if, touched with a coal like the lips of the prophet, they
would never be used for ordinary sights again.

When she finished the book, she wrote to A., "I expect
this one to be pounced on and torn limb from limb,"
but she was already thinking of a sequel. "Someday if I
get up enough courage I may write a story or a no-
vella about Tarwater in the city. . . . I would proceed
quickly to show what the children of God do to him. . . .
As Robert [Fitzgerald] says, it is the business of the artist
to uncover the strangeness of the truth. The violent are
not natural."

Many of Flannery's letters during this time are about
religion, the Church, grace, and redemption. To one friend
she wrote, "I can't allow any of my characters, in a novel
anyway, to stop in some halfway position. This doubtless
comes of a Catholic education and a Catholic sense of
history—everything works toward its true end or away
from it, everything is ultimately saved or lost." As a
Catholic living among Protestant fundamentalists, she
added, "The religion of the South is a do-it-yourself religion, something which I as a Catholic find painful and
touching and grimly comic."

To another friend, who was suffering from religious
doubt, O'Connor wrote:

> What people don't realize is how much religion costs.
> They think faith is a big electric blanket, when of course
> it is the cross. It is much harder to believe than not to
> believe. If you feel you can't believe, you must at least do
> this: keep an open mind. Keep it open toward faith, keep
> wanting it, keep asking for it, and leave the rest to God.

O'Connor had no faith, however, in reviewers. When the
novel appeared in February 1960, it received mixed reviews and, like *Wise Blood,* was widely misunderstood

by readers. To the novelist John Hawkes, she wrote in
April,

> I have been busy keeping my blood pressure down while
> reading various reviews of my book. Some of the favor-
> able ones are as bad as the unfavorable; most reviewers
> seem to have read the book in fifteen minutes and written
> the review in ten. The funniest to date was in the Savannah
> paper—Savannah, where I have innumerable kin. It was
> highly favorable, called the hero "Tarbutton" throughout
> . . . I hope that when yours comes out you'll fare better.

In the spring of 1960, Flannery received a strange re-
quest from a nun at Our Lady of Perpetual Help Free
Cancer Home in Atlanta. The nun, Sister Evangelist, wrote
to ask Flannery if she would write a memoir of a little girl
who had recently died of cancer in the home. Her letter
described Mary Ann, a girl who had been admitted to the
home as a patient in 1949 at the age of three.

> She proved to be a remarkable child and lived until she
> was twelve. Of those nine years, much is to be told.
> Patients, visitors, Sisters, all were influenced in some way
> by this afflicted child. Yet one never thought of her as
> afflicted. True she had been born with a tumor on the side
> of her face; one eye had been removed, but the other eye
> sparkled, twinkled, danced mischievously, and after one
> meeting one never was conscious of her physical defect
> but recognized only the beautiful brave spirit and felt the
> joy of such contact. Now Mary Ann's story should be
> written but who to write it?

O'Connor's first thought was "not me," but she did try to
think of a way she could help the sisters with their memoir.
She decided that "there is no quicker way to get out of a
job than to prescribe it for those who have prescribed
it for you. I added that should they decide to take my
advice, I would be glad to help them with the preparation
of their manuscript and do any small editing that proved
necessary."

O'Connor thought that would be the last she would hear of the memoir, but it was not. Sister Evangelist, who proved to be the Sister Superior of the home, began work on Mary Ann's story. In July she, five of the other sisters, a Trappist abbot, and Monsignor Dodwell visited O'Connor at Andalusia. O'Connor declared herself greatly impressed with the Sister Superior: "She is one of the funniest women I have ever encountered and has all the rock-like qualities that you would have to have to do what they do. . . . [She] is the one doing the writing on the book and she writes better than the others. She don't write like Shakespeare but she does well enough for this." O'Connor still didn't have much hope for the book itself, but her admiration for the character of Mary Ann continued to grow. "I am convinced that the child had an outsize cross and bore it with what most of us don't have and couldn't muster."

Robert Giroux, O'Connor's publisher, was well known for publishing unique books with little commercial potential. Despite this reputation, O'Connor did not expect him to accept A Memoir of Mary Ann *and lost a pair of peafowl in a bet when he did.*

O'Connor takes a stroll with some peacocks in the garden. "I am always being asked why I raise [peafowl]," she claimed, "and I have no short or reasonable answer."

Sister Evangelist gave O'Connor the finished draft of the memoir, and Flannery did what she could to polish it. In September, she wrote Robert Giroux, her publisher, to tell him about the book.

> The manuscript is not very good, of course. I set about to get the obnoxious pieties out of it and that proved almost impossible. I'm still working on it, and they are expecting me not only to turn it into a decent manuscript but to get them a publisher. Would you read it when I get it edited? I know I can't make it into the kind of thing you would publish but you might be able to tell me who might or if you think it's publishable at all.

In December 1960, she sent Giroux the corrected manuscript and told him about the titles the sisters had thought of, "some that would curl your hair. THE BRIDEGROOM COMETH, SONG WITHOUT END, THE CROOKED SMILE. The

Abbot, who is in on this too, came up with the worst: SCARRED ANGEL." Flannery convinced them that none of these titles would do, and induced them to accept the simple *A Memoir of Mary Ann,* though they complained that it was "flat."

To O'Connor's amazement, she heard from Robert Giroux within the month: his firm had accepted the memoir and would publish it in 1961. Flannery wrote him back to tell him, "the Sisters are dancing jigs all over the place. I bet them a pair of peafowl nobody would ever buy the book so I am out a pair of peafowl." To A. she confided, "I can't get over the Mary Ann business. I told the Sisters that if that child was a saint, her first miracle would be getting a publisher for their book. And now the more I think about the way that book is written, the more convinced I am that it is a genuine miracle."

But if the writing in the rest of the book is amateurish, Flannery's introduction to *A Memoir of Mary Ann* redeems it. Her introduction contains some of her best writing about the meaning of faith, of good and evil, and of the grotesque in literature. Mary Ann's deformed face, she wrote, "opened up for me a new perspective on the grotesque."

> Most of us have learned to be dispassionate about evil, to look it in the face and find, as often as not, our own grinning reflections with which we do not argue, but good is another matter. Few have stared at that long enough to accept the fact that its face too is grotesque, that in us the good is something under construction. The modes of evil usually receive worthy expression. The modes of good have to be satisfied with a cliché or a smoothing-down that will soften their real look. When we look into the face of good, we are liable to see a face like Mary Ann's, full of promise.

The sisters, delighted with the book's success and Flannery's introduction, determined to give her something "to remember them by." In March she received their gift: a television set—the first she had ever owned.

O'Connor relaxes at home at Andalusia in this 1962 photograph. By this time lupus had attacked the joints in her hips, knees, and jaw, but despite her illness, she made extensive lecture tours and wrote the stories collected in Everything That Rises Must Converge.

8

LAST YEARS

FLANNERY SPENT HER LAST YEARS writing the stories that formed her second collection, *Everything That Rises Must Converge.* The title comes from a concept described by the French theologian and paleontologist Teilhard de Chardin; he believed that all history moves toward an "omega point" at the end of time, a point at which all events merge. His most influential idea for Flannery, however, was his notion that Christians must accept the fates that befall them, no matter what they are. He called this acceptance "passive diminishment," and Flannery accepted her lupus in its light. In fact, she had come more and more to see her illness as a blessing that augmented her writing. A few years earlier she had written to A.,

> I have never been anywhere but sick. In a sense sickness is a place more
> instructive than a long trip to Europe, and it's always a place where
> there's no company, where nobody can follow. Sickness before death
> is a very appropriate thing and I think those who don't have it miss one
> of God's mercies.

Flannery certainly had her share of this dubious "blessing," which she accepted but also joked about. Her sense of irony never left her, and it is present in all of her last stories.

As Robert Fitzgerald explained, she used the title *Everything That Rises Must Converge* with both "full respect and . . . profound and necessary irony. . . . 'Rising' and 'convergence' in these stories . . . are shown in classes, generations, and colors." The title story of the collection treats the convergence of all three of these groups. Julian, an educated young man who dislikes his old-fashioned and rather silly mother, nevertheless escorts her to her weight-reducing class at the YMCA. They are traveling by bus in a Southern city, and public transportation has only recently been integrated (blacks permitted to ride side by side with whites rather than segregated in the back of the bus). Julian longs to break his mother's spirit, to break her sense that she "was someone" from a good Southern family—a white and upper-middle class family. He is embarrassed by her comments on segregation and tries to humiliate her by his chummy familiarity with blacks on the bus, who mostly ignore him.

Finally, however, a large black woman with her young son boards the bus, wearing a hat identical to the one Julian's mother has on. Julian tries to indicate her "equality" in dress to his mother, who is playing with the young boy, unaware of the stifled rage of the black mother. When they rise at the same stop, Julian's mother tries to give the boy a penny, and the boy's mother hits her with a purse and knocks her down. Julian gloats that his mother has finally received her comeuppance until he realizes she has fainted, and perhaps even is dead. Then his guilt and remorse begin, and the story ends.

Of this story, which later won first prize in the O. Henry Awards, O'Connor told Maryat Lee understatedly, it "touches on a certain topical issue in these parts and takes place on a bus." That topical issue—integration of the races—had finally been met head-on in Georgia. O'Connor noted that "most local restaurants . . . integrated peacefully" and that the local college had accepted two black students and was expecting more.

On the other hand, the final story in the collection, "Judgement Day," shows that white Southerners had a very difficult time accepting black equality. This story, which is a revision of her earliest published story, "The Geranium," portrays an old white Southern man living with his daughter in a New York City apartment. The white man tries to patronize the black tenant in the apartment next door to his, as he has always patronized blacks in the South, but his overly familiar and superior manner is insulting to this Northern black man. Tanner, the old white man, salutes the black neighbor as "Preacher," reasoning "it had been his experience that if a Negro tended to be sullen, this title usually cleared up his expression."

The neighbor feels Tanner has insulted him, particularly when the old man adds, "I reckon you wish you were back in South Alabama." The black neighbor replies, "I'm not from South Alabama. . . . I'm from New York City. And I'm not no preacher! I'm an actor." When Tanner persists in calling him "Preacher" and in patronizing him, the neighbor grabs him by the shoulders and hisses, "I don't take no crap off no wool-hat red-neck son-of-a-bitch peckerwood old bastard like you." He then flings Tanner against the wall, and the old man, in shock, has a stroke. Flannery believed firmly in equality and integration of the races, although she does not always seem "politically correct" to modern readers. For one thing, she was not ashamed of her past as an upper-middle-class white Southerner, and she, like so many of her peers, mourned the loss of the antebellum South—not its "peculiar institution" of slavery, but its rural charm and the refined manners of its citizens.

Therefore, early in 1961, she wrote a friend that she had "been vigorously celebrating Secession here—parade,

The back porch of the Andalusia farmhouse provided O'Connor with a restful place to watch the garden and her birds—and to act as a sentry in case the birds tried to eat the garden.

pageant, pilgrimages, etc." ("Secession" refers to the moment in 1861 when the Southern or Confederate states seceded, or withdrew, from the Union.) At the same time, however, she continued to have highly personal and cordial relationships with the black workers at Andalusia—Jack, Shot, and Louise—and with other blacks in the community. She noted in a letter to A.,

> I got shut of my last lecture this week and was feeling like somebody let out of the penitentiary when Regina gets a letter from her colored friend Annie that I am to write her a piece for Mother's Day at Flag Chapel (A.M.E.) entitled "Woman's Day." Last year I was summoned to write her one on "The Value of Sunday School." . . . An invite to the White House I could decline, but not this.

To another correspondent she wrote, "the radical right wing exists in pockets. There is much diversity of opinion in the South. I have just been to Texas and Southern Louisiana and I witnessed some radical conservatism and some radical liberalism too."

Flannery also felt that Southerners—blacks and whites, Protestants and Catholics—had more to unite them than

did the inhabitants of other regions of America. Southerners, she asserted, shared "a knowledge of the Bible and a
sense of history." This common ground enabled Southerners from a variety of backgrounds to feel a continuity of
experience. Flannery also believed it helped Southerners
to think in concrete rather than abstract terms—as she put
it, "We don't discuss problems; we tell stories."

In interviews and lectures at colleges Flannery continued to assert her view of the South and the Southern writer.
In April 1962, she attended the Southern Literary Festival
and met two very important Southern writers and thinkers,
Eudora Welty and Cleanth Brooks. Welty impressed her
as someone with "no pretence whatsoever, just a real nice
woman." A week later she flew to Rosary College in
Chicago, where, she said,

> the good Sisters really know how to get it out of you. I had
> 5 classes, a public lecture, read two [stories] and under-
> went a tea in which each student was determined to ask
> me an intelligent question.

Two days after that, she spoke at the University of Notre
Dame in Indiana. In June she received an honorary doctorate from St. Mary's College (an affiliate of Notre Dame),
an honor she joked about with friends.

> My degree hasn't done a thing for me so far, hasn't
> increased my self-confidence or improved my personality
> or anything I expected it to do. The local wags have
> already got tired of calling me "Doctor." Regina wrapped
> the hood up in newspaper and put it away and unless I wear
> it Halloween, I guess it'll stay there.

A year later, in June 1963, she received another honorary
degree at the Smith College commencement, where she
was also able to see Robert Fitzgerald for the first time in
three years. Regina, impressed with the honor, insisted that
they go to Boston first and round up one of her sisters and
her sister's children. Flannery drily commented that it was
like a family reunion, but "I bore up passible."

When not speaking at colleges or receiving awards, Flannery remained at home writing the stories that comprise *Everything That Rises Must Converge.* Very little mention of her disintegrating hips and jaws or her waning energy caused by the lupus enters her letters until January 1964. In one of her first letters of the year, to Maryat Lee, she wrote:

> I been sick. Fainted a few days before Christmas and was in bed about ten days and not up to much thereafter. Blood count had gone down to 8 & you can't operate on that. It's up now & so am I but aint operating yet on normal load.

In February, Flannery's doctors determined that she had a possibly malignant growth that had to be removed. She wrote to another friend, "I have a large tumor and if they dont make haste and get rid of it, they will have to remove me and leave it."

Flannery had the operation late in the month and although the fibroid tumor was successfully removed, the surgery reactivated the lupus. She remained in the hospital and in March wrote with her usual humor to A. of "an old lady across the hall from me who had been in the hospital since last November. She was about 92. Whenever they touched her, she roared LORD LORD LORD in the voice of a stevedore." In May, Flannery recovered enough to go home. She noted wistfully, "Our springs done come and gone. It is summer here." But she found happiness watching her birds. "My muscovy duck is setting under the back steps. I have two new swans who sit on the grass and converse with each other in low tones while the peacocks scream and holler."

The bout with lupus, however, left Flannery too tired to do anything other than rest in her bed. Her aunt Mary, who had recently survived a heart attack, was another guest in the house, and Flannery joked, "my parent is running the Creaking Hill Nursing Home instead of the Andalusia Cow Plantation. Or rather she is running both."

Late in May 1964, Flannery returned to the hospital for another 10-day visit. She was suffering from severe anemia, which even a series of blood transfusions seemed unable to relieve. "Prayers requested," she wrote a friend. "I am sick of being sick." On July 8, back at home but still feeling very weak, Flannery received Communion from the parish priest and also asked him for the Sacrament of the Sick. Catholics only receive this ritual anointing, once known as extreme unction, from a priest when they are in danger of dying. Flannery must have realized her end might be near. Late in July she wrote A., "I had another transfusion Wednesday but it don't seem to have done much good." The next day she wrote Maryat Lee, "I feel lousy but I dont have much idea how I really am." In her last letter to Robert Fitzgerald she wrote, "Ask Sally to pray that the lupus don't finish me off too quick." But at the end of the month of July, Flannery was rushed to the Milledgeville hospital because her kidneys had failed. She died in a coma on August 3 at the age of 39, and was buried next to her father in the Milledgeville cemetery.

* * *

Flannery O'Connor has been dead for three decades, but her novels and short stories continue to live. They have never been out of print, and she has never faded from critical consciousness. Her life was brief, but her writing continues to be influential. As Jan Nordby Gretlund noted in his preface to an important book of O'Connor criticism, *Realist of Distances,* "the full magnitude of Flannery O'Connor's genius is becoming apparent and is the subject of a growing body of criticism." Indeed, scores of books and articles have been published on Flannery O'Connor's work, even though the sum total of her published fiction comprises only two novels and two collections of short stories. Sally Fitzgerald has called the intensity of the response "an embarrassment of critical riches." As her work has become better known and more frequently taught in colleges and high schools, more and more people have

According to one observer, O'Connor's house was filled with books that "reflected the wide range of her reading" and "ornaments and icons" that showed "her interest in peacocks and her Catholicism."

come to recognize that she is the author of some of the best American fiction of the 20th century.

If, as O'Connor herself maintained, her writing has been misunderstood by the vast majority of people who read it, perhaps the enduring interest in O'Connor's work can best be explained by a passage she underlined in one

Despite O'Connor's limited output as a writer, her stories, novels, letters, and essays have been widely read and are generally considered masterpieces of American literature. Her decision— somewhat forced upon her by her illness—to keep her writing emphatically Southern helped give her a unique and personal style.

of her books, an observation by the philosopher George Santayana:

> Nothing has less to do with the real merit of a work of the imagination than the capacity of all men to appreciate it; the true test is the degree and kind of satisfaction it can give to him who appreciates it most.

The true test of the merit of Flannery O'Connor's short stories and novels is that they continue to fascinate and satisfy readers and critics alike. The true test of the merit of her life is that she worked on despite illness, never losing her sense of humor or her courage in the face of adversity.

O'Connor's deep religious faith allowed her to see her physical ailments as blessings that made her concentrate on writing. When her deteriorating health forced her to spend the rest of her life at home in Georgia, O'Connor seized the opportunity to explore the heritage and character of her region.

Not long before she died, O'Connor said of her status as a Southern writer: "To call yourself a Georgia writer is certainly to declare a limitation, but one which, like all limitations, is a gateway to reality. It is a great blessing, perhaps the greatest blessing a writer can have, to find at home what others have to go elsewhere seeking."

APPENDIX

Books by Flannery O'Connor

NOVELS

Wise Blood. New York: Farrar, Straus & Giroux, 1952.

The Violent Bear It Away. New York: Farrar, Straus & Giroux, 1960.

SHORT STORY COLLECTIONS

A Good Man Is Hard to Find. New York: Farrar, Straus & Giroux, 1955.

Everything That Rises Must Converge. New York: Farrar, Straus & Giroux, 1965.

The Complete Stories of Flannery O'Connor. New York: Farrar, Straus & Giroux, 1971.

ESSAYS

Mystery and Manners: Occasional Prose. New York: Farrar, Straus & Giroux, 1969.

LETTERS

The Habit of Being. New York: Farrar, Straus & Giroux, 1979.

COLLECTED BOOK REVIEWS

The Presence of Grace and Other Book Reviews by Flannery O'Connor. Athens: University of Georgia Press, 1983.

FURTHER READING

Asals, Frederick. *Flannery O'Connor: The Imagination of Extremity.* Athens: University of Georgia Press, 1982.

Bloom, Harold, ed. *Flannery O'Connor: Modern Critical Views.* New York: Chelsea House, 1986.

Coles, Robert. *Flannery O'Connor's South.* Baton Rouge: Louisiana State University Press, 1980.

Feeley, Kathleen. *Flannery O'Connor: The Voice of the Peacock.* New Brunswick, NJ: Rutgers University Press, 1972.

The Flannery O'Connor Bulletin. Milledgeville, GA: Georgia College, 1972–.

Guerard, Albert J., ed. *Stories of the Double.* Philadelphia: Lippincott, 1967.

Hendin, Josephine. *The World of Flannery O'Connor.* Bloomington: University of Indiana Press, 1970.

Logsdon, Loren, and Charles Mayer, eds. *Since Flannery O'Connor: Essays on the Contemporary American Short Story.* Macomb: Western Illinois University, 1987.

McKenzie, Barbara. *Flannery O'Connor's Georgia.* Athens: University of Georgia Press, 1980.

Martin, Carter W. *The True Country: Themes in the Fiction of Flannery O'Connor.* Nashville: Vanderbilt University Press, 1968.

May, John R. *The Pruning Word: The Parables of Flannery O'Connor.* Notre Dame, IN: the University of Notre Dame Press, 1976.

Muller, Gilbert H. *Nightmares and Visions: Flannery O'Connor and the Catholic Grotesque.* Athens: University of Georgia Press, 1972.

Orvell, Miles. *Invisible Parade: The Fiction of Flannery O'Connor.* Philadelphia: Temple University Press, 1972.

Ragen, Brian Abel. *A Wreck on the Road to Damascus: Innocence, Guilt, and Conversion in Flannery O'Connor.* Chicago: Loyola University Press, 1989.

Stevens, Martha. *The Question of Flannery O'Connor.* Baton Rouge: Louisiana State University Press, 1973.

Westarp, Heinze, and Jan Nordby Gretlund, eds. *Realist of Distances: Flannery O'Connor Revisited.* Aarhus, Denmark: Aarhus University Press, 1987.

CHRONOLOGY

1925	Born Mary Flannery O'Connor on March 25 in Savannah, Georgia
1931	Appears on Pathé News, a New York newsreel company, with the chicken she has trained to walk backward
1938	Edward Francis O'Connor takes a job with the Federal Housing Administration in Atlanta; Regina Cline O'Connor and Flannery move into the Cline family home in Milledgeville
1941	Edward O'Connor dies of lupus erythematosus
1942	Flannery O'Connor graduates from Peabody High School
1945	Graduates from Georgia State College for Women (now Georgia College) in Milledgeville with a B.S. degree in social science; attends Iowa Writers' Workshop on a scholarship
1946	Publishes first short story, "The Geranium," in *Accent* magazine
1947	Receives an M.F.A. degree from the University of Iowa
1948–49	Resides at Yaddo, an artists' colony in Saratoga Springs, New York
1949	Moves to Ridgefield, Connecticut, in September to live with the family of Robert and Sally Fitzgerald
1950	Becomes seriously ill in December with what is later diagnosed as lupus erythematosus; returns to Milledgeville, where she is hospitalized
1951	Moves with her mother to Andalusia, the Cline family dairy farm outside of Milledgeville; Flannery begins to raise peafowl
1952	Publishes *Wise Blood,* her first novel
1953	Receives *Kenyon Review* fellowship; her story, "The Life You Save May Be Your Own," wins second prize in the O. Henry Awards; family of Polish refugees arrives in August to work at Andalusia
1954	O'Connor reappointed a Kenyon fellow; lupus begins to disintegrate her hip bones and she must use a cane when walking
1955	Publishes *A Good Man Is Hard to Find,* her first collection of short stories; appears on television program, "Galley Proof," where she is interviewed by Harvey Breit and the first scene of "The Life You Save May Be Your Own" is dramatized; begins correspondence with "A."; starts to use crutches

1956   Sells television rights to "The Life You Save May Be Your Own" to production company for $800 and buys her mother a refrigerator; realizes that she will have to use crutches permanently because of her disintegrating hips; meets playwright Maryat Lee, sister of the new president of Georgia State College for Women

1957   "The Life You Save May Be Your Own" appears on CBS in March with Gene Kelly in the title role—Flannery is not pleased with the production; gives lectures to colleges and writing groups around the country; works on her second novel, *The Violent Bear It Away.*

1958   Flies with her mother to Europe in April and sees the Fitzgeralds in Italy; visits Lourdes, France, and has an audience with the pope in Rome; takes driving lessons over the summer, but only drives when necessary

1959   Wins an $8,000 grant from the Ford Foundation

1960   Publishes *The Violent Bear It Away;* her jaws begin to disintegrate, causing pain while eating; O'Connor receives letter from Sister Evangelist of Our Lady of Perpetual Help Cancer Home asking her to write memoir about a child with a disfiguring tumor on her face; writes the introduction to *A Memoir of Mary Ann*

1961   Robert Giroux accepts *A Memoir of Mary Ann* for his publishing house, Farrar, Straus & Giroux; book appears in stores in December

1962   O'Connor's hips disintegrate further, but an operation is deemed too dangerous; *Wise Blood* reissued with a new preface by O'Connor; *Everything That Rises Must Converge* wins first place in the O. Henry Awards; O'Connor receives honorary doctorate from St. Mary's College

1963   Receives honorary doctorate at Smith College commencement; faints shortly before Christmas and spends many days in bed

1964   Examination in early February reveals fibroid tumor; operation removes the tumor but reactivates lupus; O'Connor slips into coma on August 2, and dies of kidney failure shortly after midnight on August 3

INDEX

PICTURE CREDITS

Susan Balée is the founding editor of *Northeast Corridor,* a literary magazine based at Beaver College in Glenside, Pennsylvania. She received her Ph.D. in English from Columbia University in 1992, and her essays on Southern fiction and culture as well as 19th-century British literature have appeared in a number of journals, including *The Hudson Review, The Georgia Review,* and *Victorian Literature and Culture.* Dr. Balée resides in Haverford, Pennsylvania.

Jerry Lewis is the National Chairman of the Muscular Dystrophy Association (MDA) and host of the MDA Labor Day Telethon. An internationally acclaimed comedian, Lewis began his entertainment career in New York and then performed in a comedy team with singer and actor Dean Martin from 1946 to 1956. Lewis has appeared in many films— including *The Delicate Delinquent, Rock a Bye Baby, The Bellboy, Cinderfella, The Nutty Professor, The Disorderly Orderly,* and *The King of Comedy*—and his comedy performances continue to delight audiences around the world.

John Callahan is a nationally syndicated cartoonist and the author of an illustrated autobiography, *Don't Worry, He Won't Get Far on Foot.* He has also produced three cartoon collections: *Do Not Disturb Any Further, Digesting the Child Within,* and *Do What He Says! He's Crazy!!!* He has recently been the subject of feature articles in the *New York Times Magazine,* the *Los Angeles Times Magazine,* and the Cleveland *Plain Dealer,* and has been profiled on "60 Minutes." Callahan resides in Portland, Oregon.